ETHNOLOGUE

LANGUAGE FAMILY

INDEX

TO THE THIRTEENTH EDITION OF THE ETHNOLOGUE

Joseph E. Grimes
Barbara F. Grimes

Summer Institute of Linguistics, Inc.
Dallas, Texas

Additional copies of this *Ethnologue Language Family Index,* the *Ethnologue Language Name Index,* and the *Ethnologue* itself may be obtained from

Summer Institute of Linguistics
International Academic Bookstore
7500 West Camp Wisdom Road
Dallas, Texas 75236-5699 USA

Voice	(972) 708-7404
Fax	(972) 708-7433
Internet	academic_books@sil.org
Web	http://www.sil.org

PREFACE

This is a computer produced index to the language families that are associated with the languages listed in *Ethnologue: Languages of the World,* Thirteenth Edition, 1996. For each language it gives the main name, its three-letter Language Identification Code, the country with which the language is most centrally identified, and the language family under which it is currently classified, from the most comprehensive grouping down to the smallest. From this listing the reader can go directly to the main entry in the *Ethnologue* itself, which in turn points to entries for the same language in other countries if there are any.

As in the *Ethnologue,* the criterion for listing speech varieties separately is low intelligibility, as far as that can be ascertained. Some scholars prefer to keep dialect chains and networks unbroken; it is more consistent with what we now know about such configurations, however, to partition them into optimal clusters within which intelligibility is high and between which intelligibility is low (J. Grimes 1989, 1995). The *Ethnologue* lists speech varieties that show high intelligibility with some central variety as dialects within a single entry; the dialects do not appear in this listing, but are in the *Ethnologue.*

The classification scheme used here is largely that of the Oxford University Press *International Encyclopedia of Linguistics,* William O. Bright, editor in chief, which appeared in 1992. As the co-editors for Language Identification, we worked closely with Bright, Bernard Comrie, and the other editors to achieve a reasonable representation for the *Encyclopedia* of what is known about language families of the world. The classification information in the *Ethnologue* of 1996 still reflects the scheme followed in the *Encyclopedia* fairly closely, but incorporates some more recent classifications. The *Ethnologue* goes into greater low level detail than the *Encyclopedia* for some groupings.

For Austronesian languages, the *Comparative Austronesian Dictionary,* 1995, Darrell Tryon, editor, is followed. For Afro-Asiatic languages, Omotic tentatively replaces West Cushitic and stands as a separate branch of Afro-Asiatic. Changes in other language groupings have also been entered as more recent comparative studies have become available.

We are well aware that few classifications are airtight, and that there are good arguments for other groupings. Where the information is available, we give priority to classifications based on shared structural and lexical innovations, as opposed to lexicostatistical, purely typological, or impressionistic subgroupings.

What is presented here represents the current state of our data base, not a claim to definitiveness. This should pose no problem for specialists engaged in the study of the languages concerned, though we must beg them to recognize that to include all possible proposals for classification (including their own), or to present a history of classifications, would change this from a simple reference to a very different kind of work. At the same time, we look forward to examining the arguments for what we hope will be more firmly grounded classifications with a view to a future edition.

In the area of remote comparisons we adopt a conservative stance, as is appropriate in a publication that focuses more on the branches of trees than on the roots. Not only do we omit proposals such as proto-Human and Nostratic and Amerind, but we have even kept Baltic and Slavic separate at the highest level within Indo-European, simply because the evidence at that level does not appear as clear-cut as does the evidence for other groupings at about the same level of remoteness.

Several nongenetic categories are presented along with the genetic groupings for want of a better way to fit them into the index: creole languages, pidgins, language isolates, languages that remain unclassified, deaf sign languages, and other sign languages. There are also language isolates and unclassified languages listed within genetic groupings.

As better information has become available, we have shifted some language names from where they were in earlier editions of the *Ethnologue.* Some speech varieties that had been listed as dialects under a single language are now treated as separate entries because of low intelligibility or incompatible social attitudes, and some varieties that had been listed as separate languages are now combined because of high intelligibility. Others have been merged because of earlier confusion of language names with people names and geographic names. Usually the reason for changing a main name has to do with information about which name speakers of the language itself prefer; names imposed by outsiders seem to be all too often less than complimentary.

Each page of this index begins with the highest grouping name to which the first language on that page belongs (with a few exceptions where the computer missed the highest grouping), followed by the entire pedigree from more inclusive to least inclusive groupings. Grouping names that are duplicates of the name on the line above are represented by a hyphen (-) in order to highlight the branching and in general make things easier to find. After each grouping name there is a count of the number of distinct language entries listed under that subgrouping.

The first language listed in a subgroup follows the subgrouping name and a colon on the same line, thereby conserving about thirty pages' worth of trees. The languages within a subgroup are listed in alphabetical order. So are the subgroupings within a larger grouping. This is not the general practice of comparative linguists, who often use ordering to show either geographic topology or degrees of closeness in a way that a family tree as such does not convey well; but for a general index like this one, alphabetic ordering is essential for finding things. We have followed our sources in using conventional symbols for click sounds in language names, such as /, //, !, and ", used to write names of Khoisan languages and a few others in southern Africa. A plus sign is used in place of barred "i" in language names.

TABLE OF CONTENTS

Most comprehensive classification used.

Number of entries is in parentheses.

Afro-Asiatic (371)
- Berber (29)
- - Eastern (3)
- - - Awjila-Sokna (2): AWJILAH.AUJ (Libya)
- - - - SAWKNAH.SWN (Libya)
- - - Siwa (1): SIWI.SIZ (Egypt)
- - Guanche (1): GUANCHE.GNC (Spain)
- - Northern (20)
- - - Atlas (3): JUDEO-BERBER.JBE (Israel)
- - - - TACHELHIT.SHI (Morocco)
- - - - TAMAZIGHT, CENTRAL ATLAS.TZM (Morocco)
- - - Kabyle (1): KABYLE.KYL (Algeria)
- - - Zenati (16)
- - - - East (7): DUWINNA.DUH (Tunisia)
- - - - - GHADAMÈS.GHA (Libya)
- - - - - JABAL NAFUSAH.JBN (Libya)
- - - - - JERBA.JEA (Tunisia)
- - - - - SENED.SDS (Tunisia)
- - - - - TAMEZRET.TMZ (Tunisia)
- - - - - ZUARA.ZOU (Libya)
- - - - Ghomara (1): GHOMARA.GHO (Morocco)
- - - - Mzab-Wargla (4): TAGARGRENT.OUA (Algeria)
- - - - - TAZNATIT.GRR (Algeria)
- - - - - TEMACINE TAMAZIGHT.TJO (Algeria)
- - - - - TUMZABT.MZB (Algeria)
- - - - Riff (2): SENHAJA DE SRAIR.SJS (Morocco)
- - - - - TARIFIT.RIF (Morocco)
- - - - Shawiya (1): CHAOUIA.SHY (Algeria)
- - - - Tidikelt (1): TIDIKELT TAMAZIGHT.TIA (Algeria)
- - Tamasheq (4)
- - - Northern (1): TAMAHAQ, HOGGAR.THV (Algeria)
- - - Southern (3): TAMAJEQ, AIR.THZ (Niger)
- - - - TAMAJEQ, TAHOUA.TTQ (Niger)
- - - - TAMASHEQ, KIDAL.TAQ (Mali)
- - Zenaga (1): ZENAGA.ZEN (Mauritania)
- Chadic (192)
- - Biu-Mandara (77)
- - - A (63)
- - - - A.1 (6)
- - - - - Eastern (4): BOGA.BOD (Nigeria)
- - - - - - GA'ANDA.GAA (Nigeria)
- - - - - - HWANA.HWO (Nigeria)
- - - - - - THIR.TWI (Nigeria)
- - - - - Western (2): JARA.JAF (Nigeria)
- - - - - - TERA.TER (Nigeria)
- - - - A.2 (7)
- - - - - 1 (3): BURA-PABIR.BUR (Nigeria)
- - - - - - CIBAK.CKL (Nigeria)
- - - - - - PUTAI.MFL (Nigeria)
- - - - - 2 (3): HUBA.KIR (Nigeria)
- - - - - - MARGHI CENTRAL.MAR (Nigeria)
- - - - - - MARGHI SOUTH.MFM (Nigeria)
- - - - - NGGWAHYI.NGX (Nigeria)
- - - - A.3 (4): BANA.FLI (Nigeria)
- - - - - HYA.HYA (Cameroon)
- - - - - KAMWE.HIG (Nigeria)
- - - - - PSIKYE.KVJ (Cameroon)
- - - - A.4 (9)
- - - - - Lamang (3): HEDI.TUR (Cameroon)
- - - - - - LAMANG.HIA (Nigeria)
- - - - - - MABAS.VEM (Nigeria)
- - - - - Mandara Proper (6)
- - - - - - Glavda (4): DGHWEDE.DGH (Nigeria)
- - - - - - - GEVOKO.NGS (Nigeria)
- - - - - - - GLAVDA.GLV (Nigeria)
- - - - - - - GUDUF.GDF (Nigeria)
- - - - - - Mandara (1): WANDALA.MFI (Cameroon)
- - - - - - Podoko (1): PARKWA.PBI (Cameroon)
- - - - A.5 (20): BALDAMU.BDN (Cameroon)

Afro-Asiatic (371)
- Chadic (192)
- - East (32)
- - - A (16)
- - - - A.2 (6)
- - - - - 1 (3): LELE.LLN (Chad)
- - - - - - NANCERE.NNC (Chad)
- - - - - 2 (3): GABRI.GAB (Chad)
- - - - - - KABALAI.KVF (Chad)
- - - - - - TOBANGA.TNG (Chad)
- - - - A.3 (2): KERA.KER (Chad)
- - - - - KWANG.KVI (Chad)
- - - B (16)
- - - - B.1 (12)
- - - - - 1 (6): BIDIYO.BID (Chad)
- - - - - DANGALÉAT.DAA (Chad)
- - - - - JONKOR BOURMATAGUIL.JEU (Chad)
- - - - - MAWA.MCW (Chad)
- - - - - MOGUM.MOU (Chad)
- - - - - UBI.UBI (Chad)
- - - - - 2 (3): KAJAKSE.CKQ (Chad)
- - - - - MASMAJE.MES (Chad)
- - - - - MUBI.MUB (Chad)
- - - - - BIRGIT.BTF (Chad)
- - - - - MIGAAMA.MMY (Chad)
- - - - - TORAM.TRJ (Chad)
- - - - B.2 (1): MOKULU.MOZ (Chad)
- - - - B.3 (3): BAREIN.BVA (Chad)
- - - - - SABA.SAA (Chad)
- - - - - SOKORO.SOK (Chad)
- - Masa (9): HERDÉ.HED (Chad)
- - - MARBA.MPG (Chad)
- - - MASANA.MCN (Chad)
- - - MESME.ZIM (Chad)
- - - MONOGOY.MCU (Chad)
- - - MUSEY.MSE (Chad)
- - - NGETE.NNN (Chad)
- - - PEVÉ.LME (Chad)
- - - ZUMAYA.ZUY (Cameroon)
- - Unclassified (1): AJAWA.AJW (Nigeria)
- - West (72)
- - - A (43)
- - - - A.1 (2): GWANDARA.GWN (Nigeria)
- - - - - HAUSA.HUA (Nigeria)
- - - - A.2 (19)
- - - - - Bole (11)
- - - - - Bole Proper (10): BELE.BXQ (Nigeria)
- - - - - - BOLE.BOL (Nigeria)
- - - - - - DENO.DBB (Nigeria)
- - - - - - GALAMBU.GLO (Nigeria)
- - - - - - GERA.GEW (Nigeria)
- - - - - - GERUMA.GEA (Nigeria)
- - - - - - GIIWO.KKS (Nigeria)
- - - - - - KUBI.KOF (Nigeria)
- - - - - - MAAKA.MEW (Nigeria)
- - - - - - NGAMO.NBH (Nigeria)
- - - - - Karekare (1): KAREKARE.KAI (Nigeria)
- - - - - Tangale (8)
- - - - - Dera (1): DERA.KNA (Nigeria)
- - - - - Tangale Proper (7): BILIRI.BIA (Nigeria)
- - - - - - KUPTO.KPA (Nigeria)
- - - - - - KUSHI.KUH (Nigeria)
- - - - - - KWAAMI.KSQ (Nigeria)
- - - - - - PERO.PIP (Nigeria)
- - - - - - PIYA.PIY (Nigeria)
- - - - - - TANGALE.TAN (Nigeria)
- - - - A.3 (12)
- - - - - Angas Proper (11)
- - - - - 1 (5): ANGAS.ANC (Nigeria)

Afro-Asiatic (371)
- Chadic (192)
- - West (72)
- - - A (43)
- - - - A.3 (12)
- - - - - Angas Proper (11)
- - - - - - 1 (5): JORTO.JRT (Nigeria)
- - - - - - KOFYAR.KWL (Nigeria)
- - - - - - MISHIP.CHP (Nigeria)
- - - - - - MWAGHAVUL.SUR (Nigeria)
- - - - - - 2 (6): GOEMAI.ANK (Nigeria)
- - - - - - KOENOEM.KCS (Nigeria)
- - - - - - MONTOL.MTL (Nigeria)
- - - - - - PYAPUN.PCW (Nigeria)
- - - - - - TAL.TAL (Nigeria)
- - - - - - WEDU.WEU (Nigeria)
- - - - - Yiwom (1): YIWOM.GEK (Nigeria)
- - - - A.4 (9)
- - - - - Fyer (2): FYER.FIE (Nigeria)
- - - - - TAMBAS.TDK (Nigeria)
- - - - - Ron Proper (7): DAFFO-BATURA.DAM (Nigeria)
- - - - - KARFA.KBZ (Nigeria)
- - - - - KULERE.KUL (Nigeria)
- - - - - MUNDAT.MMF (Nigeria)
- - - - - RON.CLA (Nigeria)
- - - - - SHA.SCW (Nigeria)
- - - - - SHAGAWU.ROA (Nigeria)
- - - Unclassified (1): DAZA.DZD (Nigeria)
- - - B (29)
- - - - B.1 (5)
- - - - - Bade Proper (3): BADE.BDE (Nigeria)
- - - - - NGIZIM.NGI (Nigeria)
- - - - - TESHENAWA.TWC (Nigeria)
- - - - Duwai (1): DUWAI.DBP (Nigeria)
- - - - AUYOKAWA.AUO (Nigeria)
- - - - B.2 (9): DIRI.DWA (Nigeria)
- - - - - JIMBIN.JMB (Nigeria)
- - - - - KARIYA.KIL (Nigeria)
- - - - - MBURKU.BBT (Nigeria)
- - - - - MIYA.MKF (Nigeria)
- - - - - PA'A.AFA (Nigeria)
- - - - - SIRI.SIR (Nigeria)
- - - - - TSAGU.TGD (Nigeria)
- - - - - WARJI.WJI (Nigeria)
- - - - B.3 (15)
- - - - - Boghom (3): BOGHOM.BUX (Nigeria)
- - - - - KIR-BALAR.KKR (Nigeria)
- - - - - MANGAS.MAH (Nigeria)
- - - - - Eastern (1): JIMI.JMI (Nigeria)
- - - - - Guruntum (4): GURUNTUM-MBAARU.GRD (Nigeria)
- - - - - JU.JUU (Nigeria)
- - - - - TALA.TAK (Nigeria)
- - - - - ZANGWAL.ZAH (Nigeria)
- - - - - Zaar Proper (5): GEJI.GEZ (Nigeria)
- - - - - POLCI.POL (Nigeria)
- - - - - SAYA.SAY (Nigeria)
- - - - - ZARI.ZAZ (Nigeria)
- - - - - ZEEM.ZUA (Nigeria)
- - - - BARAWA.BWR (Nigeria)
- - - - DASS.DOT (Nigeria)
- - LURI.LDD (Nigeria)
- Cushitic (47)
- - Central (5)
- - - Eastern (1): XAMTANGA.XAN (Ethiopia)
- - - Northern (1): BILEN.BYN (Eritrea)
- - - Southern (2): AWNGI.AWN (Ethiopia)
- - - KUNFAL.XUF (Ethiopia)
- - - Western (1): AGAW, WESTERN.QIM (Ethiopia)

Afro-Asiatic (371)
- Omotic (28)
- - North (24)
- - - Gonga-Gimojan (17)
- - - - Gonga (4)
- - - - - South (2): SHAKACHO.MOY (Ethiopia)
- - - Mao (4)
- - - - East (1): BAMBASSI.MYF (Ethiopia)
- - - - West (3): GANZA.GZA (Ethiopia)
- - - - - HOZO.HOZ (Ethiopia)
- - - - - SEZE.SZE (Ethiopia)
- - South (4): AARI.AIZ (Ethiopia)
- - - DIME.DIM (Ethiopia)
- - - HAMER-BANNA.AMF (Ethiopia)
- - - KARO.KXH (Ethiopia)
- Semitic (73)
- - Central (55)
- - - Aramaic (16)
- - - - Eastern (14)
- - - - - Central (11)
- - - - - - Northeastern (9): ASSYRIAN NEO-ARAMAIC.AII (Iraq)
- - - - - - - CHALDEAN NEO-ARAMAIC.CLD (Iraq)
- - - - - - - HÉRTEVIN.HRT (Turkey)
- - - - - - - HULAULÁ.HUY (Israel)
- - - - - - - KOI-SANJAQ SOORET.KQD (Iraq)
- - - - - - - LISHANA DENI.LSD (Israel)
- - - - - - - LISHANÁN.TRG (Israel)
- - - - - - - LISHANID NOSHAN.AIJ (Israel)
- - - - - - - SENAYA.SYN (Iran)
- - - - - - Northwestern (2): MLAHSÓ.QMQ (Syria)
- - - - - - - TUROYO.SYR (Turkey)
- - - - - Mandaic (2): MANDAIC, CLASSICAL.MYZ (Iran)
- - - - - - MANDAIC.MID (Iran)
- - - - - SYRIAC.SYC (Turkey)
- - - - Western (2): SAMARITAN ARAMAIC.SRA (Palestinian West Bank and Gaza)
- - - - - WESTERN NEO-ARAMAIC.AMW (Syria)
- - - South (39)
- - - - Arabic (36): ARABIC, ALGERIAN SAHARAN SPOKEN.AAO (Algeria)
- - - - - ARABIC, ALGERIAN SPOKEN.ARQ (Algeria)
- - - - - ARABIC, BAHARNA SPOKEN.AFH (Bahrain)
- - - - - ARABIC, CHADIAN SPOKEN.SHU (Chad)
- - - - - ARABIC, CYPRIOT SPOKEN.ACY (Cyprus)
- - - - - ARABIC, DHOFARI SPOKEN.ADF (Oman)
- - - - - ARABIC, EGYPTIAN SPOKEN.ARZ (Egypt)
- - - - - ARABIC, GULF SPOKEN.AFB (Iraq)
- - - - - ARABIC, HADRAMI SPOKEN.AYH (Yemen)
- - - - - ARABIC, HASSANIYA.MEY (Mauritania)
- - - - - ARABIC, HIJAZI SPOKEN.ACW (Saudi Arabia)
- - - - - ARABIC, JUDEO-IRAQI.YHD (Israel)
- - - - - ARABIC, JUDEO-MOROCCAN.AJU (Israel)
- - - - - ARABIC, JUDEO-TRIPOLITANIAN.YUD (Israel)
- - - - - ARABIC, JUDEO-TUNISIAN.AJT (Israel)
- - - - - ARABIC, JUDEO-TUNISIAN.AJT (Tunisia)
- - - - - ARABIC, JUDEO-YEMENI.JYE (Israel)
- - - - - ARABIC, LIBYAN SPOKEN.AYL (Libya)
- - - - - ARABIC, MESOPOTAMIAN SPOKEN.ACM (Iraq)
- - - - - ARABIC, MOROCCAN SPOKEN.ARY (Morocco)
- - - - - ARABIC, NAJDI SPOKEN.ARS (Saudi Arabia)
- - - - - ARABIC, NORTH LEVANTINE SPOKEN.APC (Syria)
- - - - - ARABIC, NORTH MESOPOTAMIAN SPOKEN.AYP (Iraq)
- - - - - ARABIC, NORTHEAST EGYPTIAN BEDAWI SPOKEN.AVL (Egypt)
- - - - - ARABIC, OMANI SPOKEN.ACX (Oman)
- - - - - ARABIC, S<IDI SPOKEN.AEC (Egypt)
- - - - - ARABIC, SANAANI SPOKEN.AYN (Yemen)
- - - - - ARABIC, SHIHHI SPOKEN.SSH (United Arab Emirates)
- - - - - ARABIC, SOUTH LEVANTINE SPOKEN.AJP (Jordan)
- - - - - ARABIC, STANDARD.ABV (Saudi Arabia)
- - - - - ARABIC, SUDANESE SPOKEN.APD (Sudan)
- - - - - ARABIC, TA'IZZI-ADENI.ACQ (Yemen)

Afro-Asiatic (371)
- Semitic (73)
- - Central (55)
- - - South (39)
- - - - Arabic (36): ARABIC, TAJIKI SPOKEN.ABH (Tajikistan)
- - - - - ARABIC, TUNISIAN SPOKEN.AEB (Tunisia)
- - - - - JAKATI.JAT (Moldova)
- - - - - MALTESE.MLS (Malta)
- - - - Canaanite (3): HEBREW, ANCIENT.HBO (Israel)
- - - - - HEBREW.HBR (Israel)
- - - - - SAMARITAN.SMP (Palestinian West Bank and Gaza)
- - South (18)
- - - Ethiopian (12)
- - - - North (3): GEEZ.GEE (Ethiopia)
- - - - - TIGRÉ.TIE (Eritrea)
- - - - - TIGRINYA.TGN (Ethiopia)
- - - - South (9)
- - - - - Outer (3)
- - - - - - n-Group (2): GAFAT.GFT (Ethiopia)
- - - - - - - GURAGE, NORTH.GRU (Ethiopia)
- - - - - - tt-Group (1): GURAGE, WEST.GUY (Ethiopia)
- - - - - Transversal (6): AMHARIC.AMH (Ethiopia)
- - - - - - ARGOBBA.AGJ (Ethiopia)
- - - - - - GURAGE, EAST.GRE (Ethiopia)
- - - - - - HARARI.HAR (Ethiopia)
- - - - - - MESMES.MYS (Ethiopia)
- - - - - - ZAY.ZWA (Ethiopia)
- - - South Arabian (6): BATHARI.BHE (Oman)
- - - - HARSUSI.HSS (Oman)
- - - - HOBYOT.HOH (Oman)
- - - - JIBBALI.SHV (Oman)
- - - - MEHRI.MHR (Oman)
- - - - SOQOTRI.SQT (Yemen)
- Unclassified (1): BIRALE.BXE (Ethiopia)

Alacalufan (2): KAKAUHUA.KBF (Chile)
- KAWESQAR.ALC (Chile)

Algic (33)
- Algonquian (31)
- - Central (16)
- - - Cree (6): ATIKAMEKW.TET (Canada)
- - - - CREE, CENTRAL.CRM (Canada)
- - - - CREE, COASTAL EASTERN.CRL (Canada)
- - - - CREE, INLAND EASTERN.CRE (Canada)
- - - - CREE, WESTERN.CRP (Canada)
- - - - MONTAGNAIS.MOE (Canada)
- - - Ojibwa (4): ALGONQUIN.ALG (Canada)
- - - - OJIBWA, EASTERN.OJG (Canada)
- - - - OJIBWA, NORTHERN.OJB (Canada)
- - - - OJIBWA, WESTERN.OJI (Canada)
- - - KIKAPOO.KIC (USA)
- - - MENOMINI.MEZ (USA)
- - - MESQUAKIE.SAC (USA)
- - - MIAMI.MIA (USA)
- - - POTAWATOMI.POT (USA)
- - - SHAWNEE.SJW (USA)
- - Eastern (10): ABNAKI-PENOBSCOT.ABE (USA)
- - - MALECITE-PASSAMAQUODDY.MAC (Canada)
- - - MICMAC.MIC (Canada)
- - - MOHEGAN-MONTAUK-NARRAGANSETT.MOF (USA)
- - - MUNSEE.UMU (Canada)
- - - NANTICOKE.NNT (USA)
- - - NASKAPI.NSK (Canada)
- - - POWHATAN.PIM (USA)
- - - UNAMI.DEL (USA)
- - - WAMPANOAG.WAM (USA)
- - Plains (4)
- - - Arapaho (2): ARAPAHO.ARP (USA)

Algic (33)
- Algonquian (31)
- - Plains (4)
- - - Arapaho (2): GROS VENTRE.ATS (USA)
- - - BLACKFOOT.BLC (Canada)
- - - CHEYENNE.CHY (USA)
- - Unclassified (1): LUMBEE.LUA (USA)
- Wiyot (1): WIYOT.WIY (USA)
- Yurok (1): YUROK.YUR (USA)

Altaic (65)
- Mongolian (13)
- - Eastern (12)
- - - Dagur (1): DAUR.DTA (China)
- - - Mongour (4): BONAN.PEH (China)
- - - - DONGXIANG.SCE (China)
- - - - TU.MJG (China)
- - - - YUGUR, EAST.YUY (China)
- - - Oirat-Khalkha (7)
- - - - Khalkha-Buriat (5)
- - - - - Buriat (3): BURIAT, CHINA.BXU (China)
- - - - - - BURIAT, MONGOLIA.BXM (Mongolian Peoples Republic)
- - - - - - BURIAT, RUSSIA.MNB (Russia, Asia)
- - - - - Mongolian Proper (2): MONGOLIAN, HALH.KHK (Mongolian Peoples Republic)
- - - - - - MONGOLIAN, PERIPHERAL.MVF (China)
- - - - Oirat-Kalmyk-Darkhat (2): DARKHAT.DAY (Mongolian Peoples Republic)
- - - - - KALMYK-OIRAT.KGZ (Russia, Europe)
- - Western (1): MOGHOLI.MLG (Afghanistan)
- Tungus (12)
- - Northern (4)
- - - Even (1): EVEN.EVE (Russia, Asia)
- - - Evenki (2): EVENKI.EVN (Russia, Asia)
- - - - OROQEN.ORH (China)
- - - Negidal (1): NEGIDAL.NEG (Russia, Asia)
- - Southern (8)
- - - Southeast (5)
- - - - Nanaj (3): NANAI.GLD (Russia, Asia)
- - - - - OROK.OAA (Russia, Asia)
- - - - - ULCH.ULC (Russia, Asia)
- - - - Udihe (2): OROCH.OAC (Russia, Asia)
- - - - - UDIHE.UDE (Russia, Asia)
- - - Southwest (3): JURCHEN.JUC (China)
- - - - MANCHU.MJF (China)
- - - - XIBE.SJO (China)
- Turkic (40)
- - Bolgar (1): CHUVASH.CJU (Russia, Europe)
- - Eastern (7): AINU.AIB (China)
- - - CHAGATAI.CGT (Turkmenistan)
- - - ILI TURKI.ILI (China)
- - - UYGHUR.UIG (China)
- - - UZBEK, NORTHERN.UZB (Uzbekistan)
- - - UZBEK, SOUTHERN.UZS (Afghanistan)
- - - YUGUR, WEST.YBE (China)
- - Northern (8): ALTAI, NORTHERN.ATV (Russia, Asia)
- - - ALTAI, SOUTHERN.ALT (Russia, Asia)
- - - DOLGAN.DLG (Russia, Asia)
- - - KARAGAS.KIM (Russia, Asia)
- - - KHAKAS.KJH (Russia, Asia)
- - - SHOR.CJS (Russia, Asia)
- - - TUVIN.TUN (Russia, Asia)
- - - YAKUT.UKT (Russia, Asia)
- - Southern (12)
- - - Azerbaijani (5): AZERBAIJANI, NORTH.AZE (Azerbaijan)
- - - - AZERBAIJANI, SOUTH.AZB (Iran)
- - - - KHALAJ.KLJ (Iran)
- - - - QASHQA'.QSQ (Iran)
- - - - SALCHUQ.SLQ (Iran)
- - - Turkish (4): BALKAN GAGAUZ TURKISH.BGX (Turkey)
- - - - GAGAUZ.GAG (Moldova)

Altaic (65)
- Turkic (40)
- - Southern (12)
- - - Turkish (4): KHORASANI TURKISH.KMZ (Iran)
- - - - TURKISH.TRK (Turkey)
- - - Turkmenian (1): TURKMEN.TCK (Turkmenistan)
- - - CRIMEAN TURKISH.CRH (Uzbekistan)
- - - SALAR.SLR (China)
- - Western (11)
- - - Aralo-Caspian (4): KARAKALPAK.KAC (Uzbekistan)
- - - - KAZAKH.KAZ (Kazakhstan)
- - - - KIRGHIZ.KDO (Kyrghyzstan)
- - - - NOGAI.NOG (Russia, Europe)
- - - Ponto-Caspian (4): JUDEO-CRIMEAN TATAR.JCT (Uzbekistan)
- - - - KARACHAY-BALKAR.KRC (Russia, Europe)
- - - - KARAIM.KDR (Lithuania)
- - - - KUMYK.KSK (Russia, Europe)
- - - Uralian (3): BASHKIR.BXK (Russia, Asia)
- - - - CHULYM.CHU (Russia, Asia)
- - - - TATAR.TTR (Russia, Europe)
- - URUM.UUM (Georgia)

Amto-Musan (2): AMTO.AMT (Papua New Guinea)
- MUSAN.MMP (Papua New Guinea)

Andamanese (13)
- Great Andamanese (10)
- - Central (6): A-PUCIKWAR.APQ (India)
- - - AKA-BEA.ACE (India)
- - - AKA-KEDE.AKX (India)
- - - AKA-KOL.AKY (India)
- - - AKAR-BALE.ACL (India)
- - - OKO-JUWOI.OKJ (India)
- - Northern (4): AKA-BO.AKM (India)
- - - AKA-CARI.ACI (India)
- - - AKA-JERU.AKJ (India)
- - - AKA-KORA.ACK (India)
- South Andamanese (3): JARAWA.ANQ (India)
- - ÖNGE.OON (India)
- - SENTINEL.STD (India)

Araucanian (2): HUILLICHE.HUH (Chile)
- MAPUDUNGUN.ARU (Chile)

Arawakan (74)
- Arauan (8): ARUA.ARA (Brazil)
- - BANAWÁ.BNH (Brazil)
- - CULINA.CUL (Brazil)
- - DENÍ.DAN (Brazil)
- - JAMAMADÍ.JAA (Brazil)
- - JARUÁRA.JAP (Brazil)
- - PAUMARÍ.PAD (Brazil)
- - SURUAHÁ.SWX (Brazil)
- Guahiban (5): CUIBA.CUI (Colombia)
- - GUAHIBO.GUH (Colombia)
- - GUAYABERO.GUO (Colombia)
- - MACAGUÁN.MBN (Colombia)
- - PLAYERO.GOB (Colombia)
- Harakmbet (2): AMARAKAERI.AMR (Peru)
- - HUACHIPAERI.HUG (Peru)
- Maipuran (53)
- - Central Maipuran (6): MEHINÁKU.MMH (Brazil)
- - - PARECÍS.PAB (Brazil)
- - - SALUMÃ.UNK (Brazil)
- - - SARAVECA.SAR (Bolivia)
- - - WAURÁ.WAU (Brazil)
- - - YAWALAPITÍ.YAW (Brazil)
- - Eastern Maipuran (1): PALIKÚR.PAL (Brazil)
- - Northern Maipuran (23)

Australian (257)
- Daly (19)
- - Bringen-Wagaydy (13)
- - - Bringen (7): MARIMANINDJI.ZMM (Australia)
- - - - MARINGARR.ZMT (Australia)
- - - - MARITHIEL.MFR (Australia)
- - - - MARIYEDI.ZMY (Australia)
- - - Wagaydy (6): AMI.AMY (Australia)
- - - - GIYUG.GIY (Australia)
- - - - KUWAMA.QKU (Australia)
- - - - MANDA.ZMA (Australia)
- - - - MARANUNGGU.ZMR (Australia)
- - - - WADJIGINY.WDJ (Australia)
- - Malagmalag (4)
- - - Daly Proper (2): KAMU.QKY (Australia)
- - - - MADNGELE.ZML (Australia)
- - - Malagmalag Proper (2): MULLUKMULLUK.MPB (Australia)
- - - - TYARAITY.WOA (Australia)
- - Moil (1): NANGIKURRUNGGURR.NAM (Australia)
- - Murrinh-Patha (1): MURRINH-PATHA.MWF (Australia)
- Djamindjungan (2): DJAMINDJUNG.DJD (Australia)
- - NUNGALI.NUG (Australia)
- Djeragan (3)
- - Kitjic (1): KITJA.GIA (Australia)
- - Miriwungic (2): GADJERAWANG.GDH (Australia)
- - - MIRIWUNG.MEP (Australia)
- Enindhilyagwa (1): ANINDILYAKWA.AOI (Australia)
- Gagudjuan (1): GAGADU.GBU (Australia)
- Garawan (1): GARAWA.GBC (Australia)
- Gungaraganyan (1): KUNGARAKANY.GGK (Australia)
- Gunwingguan (13)
- - Djauanic (1): DJAUAN.DJN (Australia)
- - Gunwinggic (3): GUNWINGGU.GUP (Australia)
- - - KUNBARLANG.WLG (Australia)
- - - NGALKBUN.NGK (Australia)
- - Mangarayic (1): MANGARAYI.MPC (Australia)
- - Ngalakanic (1): NGALAKAN.NIG (Australia)
- - Ngandic (1): NGANDI.NID (Australia)
- - Nunggubuan (1): NUNGGUBUYU.NUY (Australia)
- - Rembargic (1): REMBARUNGA.RMB (Australia)
- - Warayan (1): WARAY.WRZ (Australia)
- - Yangmanic (3)
- - - Nolgin (1): YANGMAN.JNG (Australia)
- - - Wagiman (1): WAGEMAN.WAQ (Australia)
- - - Yibwan (1): WARDAMAN.WRR (Australia)
- Laragiyan (2): LARAGIA.LRG (Australia)
- - WULNA.WUX (Australia)
- Mangerrian (3)
- - Mangerric (1): MANGERR.ZME (Australia)
- - Urninganggic (2): ERRE.ERR (Australia)
- - - URNINGANGG.URC (Australia)
- Maran (3)
- - Alawic (1): ALAWA.ALH (Australia)
- - Mara (2): MARA.MEC (Australia)
- - - WANDARANG.WND (Australia)
- Nyulnyulan (8): BAADI.BCJ (Australia)
- - DJAWI.DJW (Australia)
- - DYABERDYABER.DYB (Australia)
- - DYUGUN.DYD (Australia)
- - NIMANBUR.NMP (Australia)
- - NYIGINA.NYH (Australia)
- - NYULNYUL.NYV (Australia)
- - YAWURU.YWR (Australia)
- Pama-Nyungan (176)
- - Arandic (6)
- - - Artuya (1): GAIDIDJ.GBB (Australia)
- - - Urtwa (5): ALYAWARR.ALY (Australia)
- - - - ANDEGEREBINHA.ADG (Australia)
- - - - ANMATYERRE.AMX (Australia)

Australian (257)
- Pama-Nyungan (176)
- - Paman (44)
- - - Middle Pama (15): WIKALKAN.WIK (Australia)
- - - - WIKNGENCHERA.WUA (Australia)
- - - Norman Pama (4): AREBA.AEA (Australia)
- - - - GURDJAR.GDJ (Australia)
- - - - KUNGGARA.KVS (Australia)
- - - - KUTHANT.QKD (Australia)
- - - Northeastern Pama (3): KANJU.KBE (Australia)
- - - - KUUKU-YA'U.QKL (Australia)
- - - - UMPILA.UMP (Australia)
- - - Northern Pama (4): ALNGITH.AID (Australia)
- - - - ATAMPAYA.AMZ (Australia)
- - - - LENINGITIJ.LNJ (Australia)
- - - - URADHI.URF (Australia)
- - - Rarmul Pama (2): AGHU THARNGGALU.GGR (Australia)
- - - - THAYPAN.TYP (Australia)
- - - Southern Pama (3): AGWAMIN.AWG (Australia)
- - - - MBARA.VMB (Australia)
- - - - WAMIN.WMI (Australia)
- - - Western Pama (2): THAYORE.THD (Australia)
- - - - YIR YORONT.YIY (Australia)
- - South-West (50)
- - - Coastal Ngayarda (8): DJIWARLI.DJL (Australia)
- - - - KARIYARRA.VKA (Australia)
- - - - KURRAMA.VKU (Australia)
- - - - MARTUYHUNIRA.VMA (Australia)
- - - - NGARLUMA.NRL (Australia)
- - - - NHUWALA.NHF (Australia)
- - - - PINIGURA.PNV (Australia)
- - - - YINDJIBARNDI.YIJ (Australia)
- - - Inland Ngayarda (5): NGARLA.NLR (Australia)
- - - - NYAMAL.NLY (Australia)
- - - - PANYTYIMA.PNW (Australia)
- - - - TJURRURU.TJU (Australia)
- - - - WARIYANGGA.WRI (Australia)
- - - Kanyara (4): BAYUNGU.BXJ (Australia)
- - - - BURDUNA.BXN (Australia)
- - - - DHALANDJI.DHL (Australia)
- - - - DHARGARI.DHR (Australia)
- - - Kardu (2): MALGANA.VML (Australia)
- - - - YINGGARDA.YIA (Australia)
- - - Marngu (3): KARADJERI.GBD (Australia)
- - - - MANGALA.MEM (Australia)
- - - - NYANGUMARTA.NNA (Australia)
- - - Mirning (2): KALARKO.KBA (Australia)
- - - - NGADJUNMAYA.NJU (Australia)
- - - Ngarga (2): WARLMANPA.WRL (Australia)
- - - - WARLPIRI.WBP (Australia)
- - - Ngumbin (5): GURINJI.GUE (Australia)
- - - - JARU.DDJ (Australia)
- - - - MUDBURA.MWD (Australia)
- - - - NGARINMAN.NBJ (Australia)
- - - - WALMAJARRI.WMT (Australia)
- - - Nyungar (1): NYUNGA.NYS (Australia)
- - - Wadjari (1): WATJARI.WBV (Australia)
- - - Wati (13): ANTAKARINYA.ANT (Australia)
- - - - KOKATA.KTD (Australia)
- - - - KUKATJA.KUX (Australia)
- - - - MARTU WANGKA.MPJ (Australia)
- - - - NGAANYATJARRA.NTJ (Australia)
- - - - NIJADALI.NAD (Australia)
- - - - PINI.PII (Australia)
- - - - PINTIINI.PTI (Australia)
- - - - PINTUPI-LURITJA.PIU (Australia)
- - - - PITJANTJATJARA.PJT (Australia)
- - - - WANMAN.WBT (Australia)
- - - - WIRANGU.WIW (Australia)

Australian (257)
- Pama-Nyungan (176)
- - South-West (50)
- - - Wati (13): YANKUNTATJARA.KDD (Australia)
- - - Yura (4): ADYNYAMATHANHA.ADT (Australia)
- - - - BANGGARLA.BJB (Australia)
- - - - NARUNGGA.NNR (Australia)
- - - - NUGUNU.NNV (Australia)
- - Tangic (4): GANGGALIDA.GCD (Australia)
- - - GAYARDILT.GYD (Australia)
- - - LARDIL.LBZ (Australia)
- - - NYANGGA.NNY (Australia)
- - Wagaya-Warluwaric (3)
- - - Wagaya (1): WAGAYA.WGA (Australia)
- - - Warluwara-Thawa (2): WARLUWARA.WRB (Australia)
- - - - YINDJILANDJI.YIL (Australia)
- - Waka-Kabic (4)
- - - Kingkel (1): BAYALI.BJY (Australia)
- - - Miyan (2): WAKAWAKA.WKW (Australia)
- - - - WULIWULI.WLU (Australia)
- - - Than (1): GURENG GURENG.GNR (Australia)
- - Warumungic (1): WARUMUNGU.WRM (Australia)
- - Wiradhuric (3): KAMILAROI.KLD (Australia)
- - - WANGAAYBUWAN-NGIYAMBAA.WYB (Australia)
- - - WIRADHURI.WRH (Australia)
- - Yalandyic (4): DJANGUN.DJF (Australia)
- - - GUGUYIMIDJIR.KKY (Australia)
- - - KUKU-YALANJI.GVN (Australia)
- - - MULURIDYI.VMU (Australia)
- - Yanyuwan (1): YANYUWA.JAO (Australia)
- - Yidinic (2): DYAABUGAY.DYY (Australia)
- - - YIDINY.YII (Australia)
- - Yuin-Kuric (7)
- - - Kuri (5): AWABAKAL.AWK (Australia)
- - - - DYANGADI.DYN (Australia)
- - - - NGANYAYWANA.NYX (Australia)
- - - - WORIMI.KDA (Australia)
- - - - YUGAMBAL.YUB (Australia)
- - - Yuin (2): DHURGA.DHU (Australia)
- - - - THURAWAL.TBH (Australia)
- - Yuulngu (10)
- - - Dhuwal (2): DHUWAL.DUJ (Australia)
- - - - DJAMBARRPUYNGU.DJR (Australia)
- - - Dhuwala (2): GUMATJ.GNN (Australia)
- - - - GUPAPUYNGU.GUF (Australia)
- - - DAYI.DAX (Australia)
- - - DHANGU.GLA (Australia)
- - - DJINANG.DJI (Australia)
- - - DJINBA.DJB (Australia)
- - - JARNANGO.JAY (Australia)
- - - RITARUNGO.RIT (Australia)
- Tiwian (1): TIWI.TIW (Australia)
- Unclassified (3): LIMILNGAN.LMC (Australia)
- - NGURMBUR.NRX (Australia)
- - UMBUGARLA.UMR (Australia)
- West Barkly (3)
- - Jingalic (1): DJINGILI.JIG (Australia)
- - Wambayan (2): NGARNDJI.NJI (Australia)
- - - WAMBAYA.WMB (Australia)
- Wororan (7)
- - Ungarinjinic (2): NGARINYIN.UNG (Australia)
- - - WILAWILA.WIL (Australia)
- - Wororic (1): WORORA.UNP (Australia)
- - Wunambalic (4): GAMBERA.GMA (Australia)
- - - KWINI.GWW (Australia)
- - - MIWA.VMI (Australia)
- - - WUNAMBAL.WUB (Australia)
- Yiwaidjan (4)
- - Amaragic (1): AMARAG.AMG (Australia)

Australian (257)
- Yiwaidjan (4)
- - Margic (1): MARGU.MHG (Australia)
- - Yiwaidjic (2): IWAIDJA.IBD (Australia)
- - - MAUNG.MPH (Australia)

Austro-Asiatic (180)
- Mon-Khmer (156)
- - Aslian (19)
- - - Jah Hut (1): JAH HUT.JAH (Malaysia, Peninsular)
- - - North Aslian (9)
- - - - Chewong (1): CHEWONG.CWG (Malaysia, Peninsular)
- - - - Eastern (4): BATEK.BTQ (Malaysia, Peninsular)
- - - - - JEHAI.JHI (Malaysia, Peninsular)
- - - - - MINRIQ.MNQ (Malaysia, Peninsular)
- - - - - MINTIL.MZT (Malaysia, Peninsular)
- - - - Tonga (1): TONGA.TNZ (Thailand)
- - - - Western (3): KENSIU.KNS (Malaysia, Peninsular)
- - - - - KINTAQ.KNQ (Malaysia, Peninsular)
- - - - - SEMANG, LOWLAND.ORB (Indonesia, Sumatra)
- - - Senoic (5): LANOH.LNH (Malaysia, Peninsular)
- - - - SABÜM.SBO (Malaysia, Peninsular)
- - - - SEMAI.SEA (Malaysia, Peninsular)
- - - - SEMNAM.SSM (Malaysia, Peninsular)
- - - - TEMIAR.TMH (Malaysia, Peninsular)
- - - South Aslian (4): BESISI.MHE (Malaysia, Peninsular)
- - - - SEMAQ BERI.SZC (Malaysia, Peninsular)
- - - - SEMELAI.SZA (Malaysia, Peninsular)
- - - - TEMOQ.TMO (Malaysia, Peninsular)
- - Eastern Mon-Khmer (69)
- - - Bahnaric (37)
- - - - Central Bahnaric (5): ALAK 1.ALK (Laos)
- - - - - BAHNAR.BDQ (Viet Nam)
- - - - - LAMAM.LMM (Cambodia)
- - - - - ROMAM.ROH (Viet Nam)
- - - - - TAMPUAN.TPU (Cambodia)
- - - - North Bahnaric (14)
- - - - - East (3)
- - - - - - Cua-Kayong (2): CUA.CUA (Viet Nam)
- - - - - - - KAYONG.KXY (Viet Nam)
- - - - - - Takua (1): TAKUA.TKZ (Viet Nam)
- - - - - Unclassified (1): KATUA.KTA (Viet Nam)
- - - - - West (10)
- - - - - - Duan (1): HALANG DOAN.HLD (Viet Nam)
- - - - - - Jeh-Halang (2): HALANG.HAL (Viet Nam)
- - - - - - - JEH.JEH (Viet Nam)
- - - - - - Rengao (1): RENGAO.REN (Viet Nam)
- - - - - - Sedang-Todrah (4)
- - - - - - - Sedang (2): HRE.HRE (Viet Nam)
- - - - - - - - SEDANG.SED (Viet Nam)
- - - - - - - Todrah-Monom (2): MONOM.MOO (Viet Nam)
- - - - - - - - TODRAH.TDR (Viet Nam)
- - - - - - Unclassified (2): TALIENG.TDF (Laos)
- - - - - - - TRIENG.STG (Viet Nam)
- - - - South Bahnaric (7)
- - - - - Sre-Mnong (5)
- - - - - - Mnong (3)
- - - - - - - Eastern Mnong (1): MNONG, EASTERN.MNG (Viet Nam)
- - - - - - - Southern-Central Mnong (2): MNONG, CENTRAL.MNC (Viet Nam)
- - - - - - - - MNONG, SOUTHERN.MNN (Viet Nam)
- - - - - - Sre (2): KOHO.KPM (Viet Nam)
- - - - - - - MAA.CMA (Viet Nam)
- - - - - Stieng-Chrau (2): CHRAU.CHR (Viet Nam)
- - - - - - STIENG.STI (Viet Nam)
- - - - West Bahnaric (11)
- - - - - Brao-Kravet (4): BRAO.BRB (Laos)
- - - - - - KRAVET.KRV (Cambodia)
- - - - - - KRU'NG 2.KRR (Cambodia)
- - - - - - SOU.SQQ (Laos)

Austro-Asiatic (180)
- Mon-Khmer (156)
- - Northern Mon-Khmer (38)
- - - Khmuic (13)
- - - - Mal-Khmu' (7)
- - - - - Mal-Phrai (4): LUA'.PRB (Thailand)
- - - - - - MAL.MLF (Laos)
- - - - - - PHAI.PRT (Thailand)
- - - - - - PRAY 3.PRY (Thailand)
- - - - - Mlabri (1): MLABRI.MRA (Thailand)
- - - - Xinh Mul (3): KHANG.KJM (Viet Nam)
- - - - - PONG 3.PNX (Laos)
- - - - - PUOC.PUO (Viet Nam)
- - - Mang (1): MANG.MGA (Viet Nam)
- - - Palaungic (21)
- - - - Eastern Palaungic (6)
- - - - - Danau (1): DANAU.DNU (Myanmar)
- - - - - Palaung (3): PALAUNG, PALE.PCE (Myanmar)
- - - - - - PALAUNG, RUMAI.RBB (Myanmar)
- - - - - - PALAUNG, SHWE.SWE (Myanmar)
- - - - - Riang (2): RIANG.RIL (Myanmar)
- - - - - - YINCHIA.YIN (Myanmar)
- - - - Western Palaungic (15)
- - - - - Angkuic (8): HU.HUO (China)
- - - - - - KIORR.XKO (Laos)
- - - - - - KON KEU.ANG (China)
- - - - - - MAN MET.MML (China)
- - - - - - MOK.MQT (Thailand)
- - - - - - SAMTAO.STU (Myanmar)
- - - - - - TAI LOI.TLQ (Myanmar)
- - - - - - U.UUU (China)
- - - - - Lametic (2): CON.CNO (Laos)
- - - - - - LAMET.LBN (Laos)
- - - - - Waic (5)
- - - - - - Bulang (1): BLANG.BLR (China)
- - - - - - Lawa (2): LAWA, EASTERN.LWL (Thailand)
- - - - - - - LAWA, WESTERN.LCP (China)
- - - - - - Wa (2): PARAUK.PRK (Myanmar)
- - - - - - - VO.WBM (Myanmar)
- - Palyu (1): PALYU.PLY (China)
- - Unclassified (4): BUGAN.BBH (China)
- - - BUXINHUA.BXT (China)
- - - KEMIEHUA.KFJ (China)
- - - KUANHUA.QAK (China)
- - Viet-Muong (17)
- - - Chut (5): AREM.AEM (Viet Nam)
- - - - MAY.MVZ (Viet Nam)
- - - - PAKATAN.PKT (Laos)
- - - - RUC.RUL (Laos)
- - - - SACH.SCB (Viet Nam)
- - - Cuoi (3): HUNG.HNU (Viet Nam)
- - - - PONG 2.PGO (Laos)
- - - - TUM.TMK (Laos)
- - - Muong (5): BO.BGL (Laos)
- - - - KHA TONG LUANG.KHQ (Laos)
- - - - MUONG.MTQ (Viet Nam)
- - - - NGUÔN.NUO (Viet Nam)
- - - - PONG 1.KPN (Laos)
- - - Thavung (2): PHON SUNG.PHS (Laos)
- - - - THAVUNG.THM (Laos)
- - - Unclassified (1): THO.TOU (Viet Nam)
- - - Vietnamese (1): VIETNAMESE.VIE (Viet Nam)
- Munda (24)
- - North Munda (15)
- - - Kherwari (14)
- - - - Mundari (7): ASURI.ASR (India)
- - - - - BHUMIJ.BHM (India)
- - - - - BIRHOR.BIY (India)
- - - - - HO.HOC (India)

Austro-Asiatic (180)
- Munda (24)
- - North Munda (15)
- - - Kherwari (14)
- - - - Mundari (7): KODA.KFN (India)
- - - - - KORWA.KFP (India)
- - - - - MUNDARI.MUW (India)
- - - - Santali (4): KARMALI.KFL (India)
- - - - - MAHALI.MJX (India)
- - - - - SANTALI.SNT (India)
- - - - - TURI.TRD (India)
- - - - Unclassified (3): AGARIYA.AGI (India)
- - - - - BIJORI.BIX (India)
- - - - - KORAKU.KSZ (India)
- - - Korku (1): KORKU.KFQ (India)
- - South Munda (9)
- - - Kharia-Juang (3)
- - - - Juang (1): JUANG.JUN (India)
- - - - Kharia (2): KHARIA.KHR (India)
- - - - - MIRDHA.MJY (India)
- - - Koraput Munda (6)
- - - - Gutob-Remo-Geta' (3)
- - - - - Geta' (1): GATA'.GAQ (India)
- - - - - Gutob-Remo (2): BONDO.BFW (India)
- - - - - GADABA.GBJ (India)
- - - - Sora-Juray-Gorum (3)
- - - - - Gorum (1): PARENGA.PCJ (India)
- - - - - Sora-Juray (2): JURAY.JUY (India)
- - - - - - SORA.SRB (India)

Austronesian (1236)
- Formosan (23)
- - Atayalic (2): ATAYAL.TAY (Taiwan)
- - - TAROKO.TRV (Taiwan)
- - Paiwanic (17): AMIS, NATAORAN.AIS (Taiwan)
- - - AMIS.ALV (Taiwan)
- - - BABUZA.BZG (Taiwan)
- - - BASAY.BYQ (Taiwan)
- - - BUNUN.BNN (Taiwan)
- - - HOANYA.HON (Taiwan)
- - - KAVALAN.CKV (Taiwan)
- - - KETANGALAN.KAE (Taiwan)
- - - KULUN.KNG (Taiwan)
- - - PAIWAN.PWN (Taiwan)
- - - PAPORA.PPU (Taiwan)
- - - PAZEH.PZH (Taiwan)
- - - PYUMA.PYU (Taiwan)
- - - SAISIYAT.SAI (Taiwan)
- - - SIRAIYA.FOS (Taiwan)
- - - TAOKAS.TOA (Taiwan)
- - - THAO.SSF (Taiwan)
- - Tsouic (4)
- - - Northern (1): TSOU.TSY (Taiwan)
- - - Southern (2): KANAKANABU.QNB (Taiwan)
- - - - SAAROA.SXR (Taiwan)
- - - - RUKAI.DRU (Taiwan)
- Malayo-Polynesian (1213)
- - Central-Eastern (683)
- - - Central Malayo-Polynesian (149)
- - - - Aru (14): BARAKAI.BAJ (Indonesia, Maluku)
- - - - - BATULEY.BAY (Indonesia, Maluku)
- - - - - DOBEL.KVO (Indonesia, Maluku)
- - - - - KAREY.KYD (Indonesia, Maluku)
- - - - - KOBA.KPD (Indonesia, Maluku)
- - - - - KOLA.KVV (Indonesia, Maluku)
- - - - - KOMPANE.KVP (Indonesia, Maluku)
- - - - - LOLA.LCD (Indonesia, Maluku)
- - - - - LORANG.LRN (Indonesia, Maluku)
- - - - - MANOMBAI.WOO (Indonesia, Maluku)

Austronesian (1236)
- Malayo-Polynesian (1213)
- - Central-Eastern (683)
- - - Central Malayo-Polynesian (149)
- - - - Aru (14): MARIRI.MQI (Indonesia, Maluku)
- - - - - TARANGAN, EAST.TRE (Indonesia, Maluku)
- - - - - TARANGAN, WEST.TXN (Indonesia, Maluku)
- - - - - UJIR.UDJ (Indonesia, Maluku)
- - - - Babar (11)
- - - - - North (3): BABAR, NORTH.BCD (Indonesia, Maluku)
- - - - - - DAI.DIJ (Indonesia, Maluku)
- - - - - - DAWERA-DAWELOOR.DDW (Indonesia, Maluku)
- - - - - South (8)
- - - - - - Masela-South Babar (5): BABAR, SOUTHEAST.VBB (Indonesia, Maluku)
- - - - - - - MASELA, CENTRAL.MKH (Indonesia, Maluku)
- - - - - - - MASELA, EAST.VME (Indonesia, Maluku)
- - - - - - - MASELA, WEST.MSS (Indonesia, Maluku)
- - - - - - - SERILI.SVE (Indonesia, Maluku)
- - - - - - Southwest Babar (3): EMPLAWAS.EMW (Indonesia, Maluku)
- - - - - - - IMROING.IMR (Indonesia, Maluku)
- - - - - - - TELA-MASBUAR.TVM (Indonesia, Maluku)
- - - - Bima-Sumba (26)
- - - - - Ende-Lio (4): ENDE.END (Indonesia, Nusa Tenggara)
- - - - - - KEO.XXK (Indonesia, Nusa Tenggara)
- - - - - - LI'O.LJL (Indonesia, Nusa Tenggara)
- - - - - - NAGE.NXE (Indonesia, Nusa Tenggara)
- - - - - ANAKALANGU.AKG (Indonesia, Nusa Tenggara)
- - - - - BIMA.BHP (Indonesia, Nusa Tenggara)
- - - - - KEPO'.KUK (Indonesia, Nusa Tenggara)
- - - - - KODI.KOD (Indonesia, Nusa Tenggara)
- - - - - KOMODO.KVH (Indonesia, Nusa Tenggara)
- - - - - LAMBOYA.LMY (Indonesia, Nusa Tenggara)
- - - - - MAMBORU.MVD (Indonesia, Nusa Tenggara)
- - - - - MANGGARAI.MQY (Indonesia, Nusa Tenggara)
- - - - - NDAO.NFA (Indonesia, Nusa Tenggara)
- - - - - NGAD'A, EASTERN.NEA (Indonesia, Nusa Tenggara)
- - - - - NGAD'A.NXG (Indonesia, Nusa Tenggara)
- - - - - PALU'E.PLE (Indonesia, Nusa Tenggara)
- - - - - RAJONG.RJG (Indonesia, Nusa Tenggara)
- - - - - REMBONG.REB (Indonesia, Nusa Tenggara)
- - - - - RIUNG.RIU (Indonesia, Nusa Tenggara)
- - - - - RONGGA.ROR (Indonesia, Nusa Tenggara)
- - - - - SABU.HVN (Indonesia, Nusa Tenggara)
- - - - - SO'A.SSQ (Indonesia, Nusa Tenggara)
- - - - - SUMBA.SMI (Indonesia, Nusa Tenggara)
- - - - - WAE RANA.WRX (Indonesia, Nusa Tenggara)
- - - - - WANUKAKA.WNK (Indonesia, Nusa Tenggara)
- - - - - WEYEWA.WEW (Indonesia, Nusa Tenggara)
- - - - - Central Maluku (55)
- - - - - Ambelau (1): AMBELAU.AMV (Indonesia, Maluku)
- - - - - Buru (4): BURU.MHS (Indonesia, Maluku)
- - - - - - LISELA.LCL (Indonesia, Maluku)
- - - - - - MOKSELA.VMS (Indonesia, Maluku)
- - - - - - PALUMATA.PMC (Indonesia, Maluku)
- - - - - East (46)
- - - - - - Banda-Geser (4)
- - - - - - - Geser-Gorom (3): BATI.BVT (Indonesia, Maluku)
- - - - - - - - GESER-GOROM.GES (Indonesia, Maluku)
- - - - - - - - WATUBELA.WAH (Indonesia, Maluku)
- - - - - - - BANDA.BND (Indonesia, Maluku)
- - - - - - Seram (41)
- - - - - - - Bobot (1): BOBOT.BTY (Indonesia, Maluku)
- - - - - - - East Seram (1): HOTI.HTI (Indonesia, Maluku)
- - - - - - - Manusela-Seti (5): BENGGOI.BGY (Indonesia, Maluku)
- - - - - - - - HUAULU.HUD (Indonesia, Maluku)
- - - - - - - - LIANA-SETI.STE (Indonesia, Maluku)
- - - - - - - - MANUSELA.WHA (Indonesia, Maluku)
- - - - - - - - SALAS.SGU (Indonesia, Maluku)
- - - - - - - Masiwang (1): MASIWANG.BNF (Indonesia, Maluku)

Austronesian (1236)
- Malayo-Polynesian (1213)
- - Central-Eastern (683)
- - - Eastern Malayo-Polynesian (532)
- - - - Oceanic (493)
- - - - - Western Oceanic (231)
- - - - - - Meso Melanesian (66)
- - - - - - - New Ireland (60)
- - - - - - - - South New Ireland-Northwest Solomonic (48)
- - - - - - - - - New Georgia (10)
- - - - - - - - - - West (8): ROVIANA.RUG (Solomon Islands)
- - - - - - - - - - - SIMBO.SBB (Solomon Islands)
- - - - - - - - - - - UGHELE.UGE (Solomon Islands)
- - - - - - - - - Patpatar-Tolai (10): GURAMALUM.GRZ (Papua New Guinea)
- - - - - - - - - - KANDAS.KQW (Papua New Guinea)
- - - - - - - - - - KONOMALA.KOA (Papua New Guinea)
- - - - - - - - - - KUANUA.KSD (Papua New Guinea)
- - - - - - - - - - LABEL.LBB (Papua New Guinea)
- - - - - - - - - - PATPATAR.GFK (Papua New Guinea)
- - - - - - - - - - RAMOAAINA.RAI (Papua New Guinea)
- - - - - - - - - - SIAR.SJR (Papua New Guinea)
- - - - - - - - - - SURSURUNGA.SGZ (Papua New Guinea)
- - - - - - - - - - TANGGA.TGG (Papua New Guinea)
- - - - - - - - - Piva-Banoni (2): BANONI.BCM (Papua New Guinea)
- - - - - - - - - - PIVA.TGI (Papua New Guinea)
- - - - - - - - - Santa Isabel (7)
- - - - - - - - - - Central (3): BLABLANGA.BLP (Solomon Islands)
- - - - - - - - - - - KOKOTA.KKK (Solomon Islands)
- - - - - - - - - - - ZAZAO.JAJ (Solomon Islands)
- - - - - - - - - - East (2): CHEKE HOLO.MRN (Solomon Islands)
- - - - - - - - - - - GAO.GGA (Solomon Islands)
- - - - - - - - - - West (2): LAGHU.LGB (Solomon Islands)
- - - - - - - - - - - ZABANA.KJI (Solomon Islands)
- - - - - - - - - - BILUR.BXF (Papua New Guinea)
- - - - - - - - - Tabar (2): LIHIR.LIH (Papua New Guinea)
- - - - - - - - - - NOTSI.NCF (Papua New Guinea)
- - - - - - - - - Tomoip (1): TOMOIP.TUM (Papua New Guinea)
- - - - - - - - Willaumez (4): BOLA.BNP (Papua New Guinea)
- - - - - - - - - BULU.BJL (Papua New Guinea)
- - - - - - - - - MERAMERA.MXM (Papua New Guinea)
- - - - - - - - - NAKANAI.NAK (Papua New Guinea)
- - - - - - - North New Guinea (108)
- - - - - - - - Huon Gulf (32)
- - - - - - - - - Markham (13)
- - - - - - - - - - Lower (7)
- - - - - - - - - - - Busu (5): ARIBWATSA.LAZ (Papua New Guinea)
- - - - - - - - - - - - ARIBWAUNG.YLU (Papua New Guinea)
- - - - - - - - - - - - DUWET.GVE (Papua New Guinea)
- - - - - - - - - - - - MUSOM.MSU (Papua New Guinea)
- - - - - - - - - - - - NAFI.SRF (Papua New Guinea)
- - - - - - - - - - - Labu (1): LABU.LBU (Papua New Guinea)
- - - - - - - - - - - Wampar (1): WAMPAR.LBQ (Papua New Guinea)
- - - - - - - - - - Upper (3)
- - - - - - - - - - - Adzera (1): ADZERA.AZR (Papua New Guinea)
- - - - - - - - - - - Mountain (2): MARI.HOB (Papua New Guinea)
- - - - - - - - - - - - WAMPUR.WAZ (Papua New Guinea)
- - - - - - - - - - Watut (3): WATUT, MIDDLE.MPL (Papua New Guinea)
- - - - - - - - - - - WATUT, NORTH.UNA (Papua New Guinea)
- - - - - - - - - - - WATUT, SOUTH.MCY (Papua New Guinea)
- - - - - - - - - North (3): BUGAWAC.BUK (Papua New Guinea)
- - - - - - - - - - KELA.KCL (Papua New Guinea)
- - - - - - - - - - YABEM.JAE (Papua New Guinea)
- - - - - - - - - Numbami (1): NUMBAMI.SIJ (Papua New Guinea)
- - - - - - - - - South (15)
- - - - - - - - - - Hote-Buang (14)
- - - - - - - - - - - Buang (12)
- - - - - - - - - - - - Mumeng (7): DAMBI.DAC (Papua New Guinea)
- - - - - - - - - - - - - DENGALU.DEA (Papua New Guinea)
- - - - - - - - - - - - - GORAKOR.GOC (Papua New Guinea)

Austronesian (1236)
- Malayo-Polynesian (1213)
- - Western Malayo-Polynesian (528)
- - - Borneo (137)
- - - - Northwest (84)
- - - - - North Sarawakan (37)
- - - - - - Dayic (18)
- - - - - - - Murutic (12)
- - - - - - - - Murut (6): OKOLOD.KQV (Malaysia, Sarawak)
- - - - - - - - - PALUAN.PLZ (Malaysia, Sabah)
- - - - - - - - - SELUNGAI MURUT.SLG (Malaysia, Sabah)
- - - - - - - - - TAGAL MURUT.MVV (Malaysia, Sabah)
- - - - - - - - - TIMUGON MURUT.TIH (Malaysia, Sabah)
- - - - - - - - Northern (1): BAUKAN.BNB (Malaysia, Sabah)
- - - - - - - - Tidong (5): BOLONGAN.BLJ (Indonesia, Kalimantan)
- - - - - - - - - KALABAKAN.KVE (Malaysia, Sabah)
- - - - - - - - - SEMBAKUNG MURUT.SMA (Indonesia, Kalimantan)
- - - - - - - - - SERUDUNG MURUT.SRK (Malaysia, Sabah)
- - - - - - - - - TIDONG.TID (Indonesia, Kalimantan)
- - - - - - - Kenyah (12)
- - - - - - - - Main Kenyah (6): KENYAH, BAHAU RIVER.BWV (Indonesia, Kalimantan)
- - - - - - - - - KENYAH, KAYAN RIVER.KNH (Indonesia, Kalimantan)
- - - - - - - - - KENYAH, KELINYAU.XKL (Indonesia, Kalimantan)
- - - - - - - - - KENYAH, MAHAKAM.XKM (Indonesia, Kalimantan)
- - - - - - - - - KENYAH, UPPER BARAM.UBM (Malaysia, Sarawak)
- - - - - - - - - KENYAH, WESTERN.XKY (Malaysia, Sarawak)
- - - - - - - - Sebob (2): KENYAH, SEBOB.SIB (Malaysia, Sarawak)
- - - - - - - - - MADANG.MQD (Malaysia, Sarawak)
- - - - - - - - KENYAH, BAKUNG.BOC (Indonesia, Kalimantan)
- - - - - - - - KENYAH, TUTOH.TTW (Malaysia, Sarawak)
- - - - - - - - KENYAH, WAHAU.WHK (Indonesia, Kalimantan)
- - - - - - - - PUNAN TUBU.PUJ (Indonesia, Kalimantan)
- - - - - - - Rejang-Sajau (5): BASAP.BDB (Indonesia, Kalimantan)
- - - - - - - - BURUSU.BQR (Indonesia, Kalimantan)
- - - - - - - - PUNAN BAH-BIAU.PNA (Malaysia, Sarawak)
- - - - - - - - PUNAN MERAP.PUC (Indonesia, Kalimantan)
- - - - - - - - SAJAU BASAP.SAD (Indonesia, Kalimantan)
- - - - - - Sabahan (29)
- - - - - - - Dusunic (23)
- - - - - - - - Bisaya (5)
- - - - - - - - - Southern (3): BISAYA, BRUNEI.BSB (Brunei)
- - - - - - - - - - BISAYA, SARAWAK.BSD (Malaysia, Sarawak)
- - - - - - - - - - TUTONG 1.TTX (Brunei)
- - - - - - - - - BISAYA, SABAH.BSY (Malaysia, Sabah)
- - - - - - - - - TATANA.TXX (Malaysia, Sabah)
- - - - - - - - Dusun (17)
- - - - - - - - - Central (6): DUSUN, CENTRAL.DTP (Malaysia, Sabah)
- - - - - - - - - - DUSUN, SUGUT.KZS (Malaysia, Sabah)
- - - - - - - - - - DUSUN, TAMBUNAN.KZT (Malaysia, Sabah)
- - - - - - - - - - DUSUN, TEMPASUK.TDU (Malaysia, Sabah)
- - - - - - - - - - KOTA MARUDU TINAGAS.KTR (Malaysia, Sabah)
- - - - - - - - - - MINOKOK.MQQ (Malaysia, Sabah)
- - - - - - - - - Eastern (1): KADAZAN, LABUK-KINABATANGAN.DTB (Malaysia, Sabah)
- - - - - - - - - GANA.GNQ (Malaysia, Sabah)
- - - - - - - - - KADAZAN, COASTAL.KZJ (Malaysia, Sabah)
- - - - - - - - - KADAZAN, KLIAS RIVER.KQT (Malaysia, Sabah)
- - - - - - - - - KIMARAGANG.KQR (Malaysia, Sabah)
- - - - - - - - - KOTA MARUDU TALANTANG.GRM (Malaysia, Sabah)
- - - - - - - - - KUIJAU.DKR (Malaysia, Sabah)
- - - - - - - - - LOTUD.DTR (Malaysia, Sabah)
- - - - - - - - - PAPAR.DPP (Malaysia, Sabah)
- - - - - - - - - RUNGUS.DRG (Malaysia, Sabah)
- - - - - - - - - TEBILUNG.TGB (Malaysia, Sabah)
- - - - - - - - - Unclassified (1): DUMPAS.DMV (Malaysia, Sabah)
- - - - - - - - Ida'an (1): IDA'AN.DBJ (Malaysia, Sabah)
- - - - - - - Paitanic (5)
- - - - - - - - Upper Kinabatangan (3): KINABATANGAN, UPPER.DMG (Malaysia, Sabah)
- - - - - - - - - LOBU, LANAS.RUU (Malaysia, Sabah)
- - - - - - - - - LOBU, TAMPIAS.LOW (Malaysia, Sabah)

Austronesian (1236)
- Malayo-Polynesian (1213)
- - Western Malayo-Polynesian (528)
- - - Meso Philippine (60)
- - - - Kalamian (3): TAGBANWA, CALAMIAN.TBK (Philippines)
- - - - - TAGBANWA, CENTRAL.TGT (Philippines)
- - - - Palawano (7): BATAK.BTK (Philippines)
- - - - - BONGGI.BDG (Malaysia, Sabah)
- - - - - MOLBOG.PWM (Philippines)
- - - - - PALAWANO, BROOKE'S POINT.PLW (Philippines)
- - - - - PALAWANO, CENTRAL.PLC (Philippines)
- - - - - PALAWANO, SOUTHWEST.PLV (Philippines)
- - - - - TAGBANWA.TBW (Philippines)
- - - - South Mangyan (4)
- - - - - Buhid-Taubuid (3): BUHID.BKU (Philippines)
- - - - - - TAWBUID, EASTERN.BNJ (Philippines)
- - - - - - TAWBUID, WESTERN.TWB (Philippines)
- - - - - Hanunoo (1): HANUNOO.HNN (Philippines)
- - - Northern Philippine (70)
- - - - Bashiic-Central Luzon-Northern Mindoro (16)
- - - - - Bashiic (3)
- - - - - - Ivatan (2): IBATAN.IVB (Philippines)
- - - - - - - IVATAN.IVV (Philippines)
- - - - - - Yami (1): YAMI.YMI (Taiwan)
- - - - - Central Luzon (10)
- - - - - - Pampangan (1): PAMPANGAN.PMP (Philippines)
- - - - - - Sambalic (8): AYTA, ABENLEN.ABP (Philippines)
- - - - - - - AYTA, AMBALA.ABC (Philippines)
- - - - - - - AYTA, BATAAN.AYT (Philippines)
- - - - - - - AYTA, MAG-ANCHI.SGB (Philippines)
- - - - - - - AYTA, MAG-INDI.BLX (Philippines)
- - - - - - - BOLINAO.SMK (Philippines)
- - - - - - - SAMBAL, BOTOLAN.SBL (Philippines)
- - - - - - - SAMBAL, TINA.SNA (Philippines)
- - - - - Sinauna (1): AGTA, REMONTADO.AGV (Philippines)
- - - - - Northern Mindoro (3): ALANGAN.ALJ (Philippines)
- - - - - - IRAYA.IRY (Philippines)
- - - - - TADYAWAN.TDY (Philippines)
- - - - Northern Luzon (54)
- - - - - Alta (2): ALTA, NORTHERN.AQN (Philippines)
- - - - - - ALTA, SOUTHERN.AGY (Philippines)
- - - - - Arta (1): ARTA.ATZ (Philippines)
- - - - - Ilocano (1): ILOCANO.ILO (Philippines)
- - - - - Northern Cordilleran (20)
- - - - - - Dumagat (9)
- - - - - - - Northern (6): AGTA, CASIGURAN DUMAGAT.DGC (Philippines)
- - - - - - - - AGTA, CENTRAL CAGAYAN.AGT (Philippines)
- - - - - - - - AGTA, DICAMAY.DUY (Philippines)
- - - - - - - - AGTA, DUPANINAN.DUO (Philippines)
- - - - - - - - KASIGURANIN.KSN (Philippines)
- - - - - - - - PARANAN.AGP (Philippines)
- - - - - - - Southern (3): AGTA, ALABAT ISLAND.DUL (Philippines)
- - - - - - - - AGTA, CAMARINES NORTE.ABD (Philippines)
- - - - - - - - AGTA, UMIRAY DUMAGET.DUE (Philippines)
- - - - - - Ibanagic (11)
- - - - - - - Gaddang (2): GA'DANG.GDG (Philippines)
- - - - - - - - GADDANG.GAD (Philippines)
- - - - - - - Ibanag (7): AGTA, VILLAVICIOSA.DYG (Philippines)
- - - - - - - - ATTA, FAIRE.ATH (Philippines)
- - - - - - - - ATTA, PAMPLONA.ATT (Philippines)
- - - - - - - - ATTA, PUDTOL.ATP (Philippines)
- - - - - - - - IBANAG.IBG (Philippines)
- - - - - - - - ITAWIT.ITV (Philippines)
- - - - - - - - YOGAD.YOG (Philippines)
- - - - - - - Isnag (2): ADASEN.TIU (Philippines)
- - - - - - - - ISNAG.ISD (Philippines)
- - - - - South-Central Cordilleran (30)
- - - - - - Central Cordilleran (22)
- - - - - - - Isinai (1): ISINAI.INN (Philippines)

Austronesian (1236)
- Malayo-Polynesian (1213)
- - Western Malayo-Polynesian (528)
- - - Southern Philippine (22)
- - - - Manobo (15)
- - - - - Central (8)
- - - - - - East (3): MANOBO, DIBABAWON.MBD (Philippines)
- - - - - - MANOBO, RAJAH KABUNSUWAN.MQK (Philippines)
- - - - - - South (3)
- - - - - - - Ata-Tigwa (2): MANOBO, ATA.ATD (Philippines)
- - - - - - - MANOBO, MATIGSALUG.MBT (Philippines)
- - - - - - Obo (1): MANOBO, OBO.OBO (Philippines)
- - - - - West (2): MANOBO, ILIANEN.MBI (Philippines)
- - - - - - MANOBO, WESTERN BUKIDNON.MBB (Philippines)
- - - - - North (4): BINUKID.BKD (Philippines)
- - - - - HIGAONON.MBA (Philippines)
- - - - - KAGAYANEN.CGC (Philippines)
- - - - - MANOBO, CINAMIGUIN.MKX (Philippines)
- - - - - South (3): MANOBO, COTABATO.MTA (Philippines)
- - - - - MANOBO, SARANGANI.MBS (Philippines)
- - - - - MANOBO, TAGABAWA.BGS (Philippines)
- - - - Subanun (4)
- - - - - Eastern (3): SUBANEN, CENTRAL.SUS (Philippines)
- - - - - SUBANEN, NORTHERN.STB (Philippines)
- - - - - SUBANUN, LAPUYAN.LAA (Philippines)
- - - - Kalibugan (1): SUBANON, WESTERN.SUC (Philippines)
- - - Sulawesi (112)
- - - - Central Sulawesi (46)
- - - - - Banggai (1): BANGGAI.BGZ (Indonesia, Sulawesi)
- - - - - Eastern (4): ANDIO.BZB (Indonesia, Sulawesi)
- - - - - BALANTAK.BLZ (Indonesia, Sulawesi)
- - - - - SALUAN, COASTAL.LOE (Indonesia, Sulawesi)
- - - - - SALUAN, KAHUMAMAHON.SLB (Indonesia, Sulawesi)
- - - - - West Central (41)
- - - - - Balaesan (1): BALAESAN.BLS (Indonesia, Sulawesi)
- - - - - Bungku-Mori-Tolaki (15)
- - - - - - Bungku (5): BUNGKU.BKZ (Indonesia, Sulawesi)
- - - - - - - KORONI.XKQ (Indonesia, Sulawesi)
- - - - - - - KULISUSU.VKL (Indonesia, Sulawesi)
- - - - - - - MORONENE.MQN (Indonesia, Sulawesi)
- - - - - - - WAWONII.WOW (Indonesia, Sulawesi)
- - - - - - Mori (5): BAHONSUAI.BSU (Indonesia, Sulawesi)
- - - - - - - MORI ATAS.MZQ (Indonesia, Sulawesi)
- - - - - - - MORI BAWAH.XMZ (Indonesia, Sulawesi)
- - - - - - - PADOE.PDO (Indonesia, Sulawesi)
- - - - - - - TOMADINO.TDI (Indonesia, Sulawesi)
- - - - - - Tolaki (4): KODEOHA.VKO (Indonesia, Sulawesi)
- - - - - - - RAHAMBUU.RAZ (Indonesia, Sulawesi)
- - - - - - - TOLAKI.LBW (Indonesia, Sulawesi)
- - - - - - - WARU.WRU (Indonesia, Sulawesi)
- - - - - - TALOKI.TLK (Indonesia, Sulawesi)
- - - - - Kaili-Pamona (15)
- - - - - - Kaili (9): BARAS.BRS (Indonesia, Sulawesi)
- - - - - - - KAILI, DA'A.KZF (Indonesia, Sulawesi)
- - - - - - - KAILI, LEDO.LEW (Indonesia, Sulawesi)
- - - - - - - LINDU.KLW (Indonesia, Sulawesi)
- - - - - - - MOMA.MYL (Indonesia, Sulawesi)
- - - - - - - SARUDU.SDU (Indonesia, Sulawesi)
- - - - - - - SEDOA.TVW (Indonesia, Sulawesi)
- - - - - - - TOPOIYO.TOY (Indonesia, Sulawesi)
- - - - - - - UMA.PPK (Indonesia, Sulawesi)
- - - - - - Pamona (6): BADA.BHZ (Indonesia, Sulawesi)
- - - - - - - BESOA.BEP (Indonesia, Sulawesi)
- - - - - - - NAPU.NAP (Indonesia, Sulawesi)
- - - - - - - PAMONA.BCX (Indonesia, Sulawesi)
- - - - - - - RAMPI.LJE (Indonesia, Sulawesi)
- - - - - - - TOMBELALA.TTP (Indonesia, Sulawesi)
- - - - - Tomini (10): BOLANO.BZL (Indonesia, Sulawesi)
- - - - - - DAMPAL.DMP (Indonesia, Sulawesi)

Carib (29)
- Northern (21)
- - East-West Guiana (12)
- - - Wayana-Trio (3): TRIÓ.TRI (Surinam)
- - - - WAYANA.WAY (Surinam)
- - Galibi (1): KALIHNA.CRB (Venezuela)
- - Northern Brazil (2): ARÁRA, PARÁ.AAP (Brazil)
- - - TXIKÃO.TXI (Brazil)
- - Western Guiana (3): MAPOYO.MCG (Venezuela)
- - - PANARE.PBH (Venezuela)
- - - YABARANA.YAR (Venezuela)
- Southern (8)
- - Southeastern Colombia (1): CARIJONA.CBD (Colombia)
- - Southern Guiana (3): HIXKARYÁNA.HIX (Brazil)
- - - KAXUIÂNA.KBB (Brazil)
- - - MAQUIRITARI.MCH (Venezuela)
- - Xingu Basin (4): BAKAIRÍ.BKQ (Brazil)
- - - KUIKÚRO-KALAPÁLO.KUI (Brazil)
- - - MATIPUHY.MZO (Brazil)
- - - YARUMÁ.YRM (Brazil)

Chapacura-Wanham (5)
- Guapore (2): ITENE.ITE (Bolivia)
- - KABIXÍ.KBD (Brazil)
- Madeira (3): ORO WIN.ORW (Brazil)
- - PAKAÁSNOVOS.PAV (Brazil)
- - TORÁ.TRZ (Brazil)

Chibchan (22)
- Aruak (3): ICA.ARH (Colombia)
- - KOGUI.KOG (Colombia)
- - MALAYO.MBP (Colombia)
- Chibchan Proper (5)
- - Tunebo (4): TUNEBO, ANGOSTURAS.TND (Colombia)
- - - TUNEBO, BARRO NEGRO.TBN (Colombia)
- - - TUNEBO, CENTRAL.TUF (Colombia)
- - - TUNEBO, WESTERN.TNB (Colombia)
- - CHIBCHA.CBF (Colombia)
- Cofan (1): COFÁN.CON (Ecuador)
- Guaymi (2): BUGLERE.SAB (Panama)
- - GUAYMÍ.GYM (Panama)
- Kuna (2): KUNA, BORDER.KUA (Colombia)
- - KUNA, SAN BLAS.CUK (Panama)
- Motilon (1): MOTILÓN.MOT (Colombia)
- Paya (1): PECH.PAY (Honduras)
- Rama (2): MALÉKU JAÍKA.GUT (Costa Rica)
- - RAMA.RMA (Nicaragua)
- Talamanca (4): BORUCA.BRN (Costa Rica)
- - BRIBRI.BZD (Costa Rica)
- - CABÉCAR.CJP (Costa Rica)
- - TERIBE.TFR (Panama)
- Unclassified (1): CHIMILA.CBG (Colombia)

Chimakuan (1): QUILEUTE.QUI (USA)

Choco (10)
- Embera (6)
- - Northern (2): EMBERÁ, NORTHERN.EMP (Panama)
- - - EMBERÁ-CATÍO.CTO (Colombia)
- - Southern (4): EMBERÁ-CHAMÍ.CMI (Colombia)
- - - EMBERÁ-TADÓ.TDC (Colombia)
- - - EMBERA-BAUDÓ.BDC (Colombia)
- - - EMBERA-SAIJA.SJA (Colombia)
- ANSERMA.ANS (Colombia)
- ARMA.AOH (Colombia)
- RUNA.RUN (Colombia)
- WAUMEO.NOA (Panama)

Chon (2): ONA.ONA (Argentina)
- TEHUELCHE.TEH (Argentina)

Chukotko-Kamchatkan (5)
- Northern (4)
- - Chukot (1): CHUKOT.CKT (Russia, Asia)
- - Koryak-Alyutor (3): ALUTOR.ALR (Russia, Asia)
- - - KEREK.KRK (Russia, Asia)
- - - KORYAK.KPY (Russia, Asia)
- Southern (1): ITELMEN.ITL (Russia, Asia)

Coahuiltecan (1): TONKAWA.TON (USA)

Creole (66)
- Afrikaans based (2): FLY TAAL.FLY (South Africa)
- - OORLANS.OOR (South Africa)
- Arabic based (3): ARABIC, BABALIA CREOLE.BBZ (Chad)
- - ARABIC, SUDANESE CREOLE.PGA (Sudan)
- - NUBI.KCN (Uganda)
- Assamese based (1): NAGA PIDGIN.NAG (India)
- Cree-French (1): MITCHIF.CRG (USA)
- Dutch based (3): BERBICE CREOLE DUTCH.BRC (Guyana)
- - DUTCH CREOLE.DCR (U.S. Virgin Islands)
- - SKEPI CREOLE DUTCH.SKW (Guyana)
- English based (22)
- - Atlantic (15)
- - - Eastern (5)
- - - - Northern (3): AFRO-SEMINOLE CREOLE.AFS (USA)
- - - - - BAHAMAS CREOLE ENGLISH.BAH (Bahamas)
- - - - - SEA ISLANDS CREOLE ENGLISH.GUL (USA)
- - - - Southern (2): GUYANESE.GYN (Guyana)
- - - - - LESSER ANTILLEAN CREOLE ENGLISH.VIB (Trinidad and Tobago)
- - - Krio (3): KRIO.KRI (Sierra Leone)
- - - - PIDGIN, CAMEROON.WES (Cameroon)
- - - - PIDGIN, NIGERIAN.PCM (Nigeria)
- - - Surinam (4)
- - - - Djuka (2): AUKAANS.DJK (Surinam)
- - - - - KWINTI.KWW (Surinam)
- - - - Saramaccan (1): SARAMACCAN.SRM (Surinam)
- - - - SRANAN.SRN (Surinam)
- - - Unclassified (1): SAMANÁ ENGLISH.SAX (Dominican Republic)
- - - Western (2): BELIZE CREOLE ENGLISH.BZI (Belize)
- - - - WESTERN CARIBBEAN CREOLE ENGLISH.JAM (Jamaica)
- - Pacific (7): BISLAMA.BCY (Vanuatu)
- - - HAWAI'I CREOLE ENGLISH.HAW (USA)
- - - KRIOL.ROP (Australia)
- - - NGATIK MEN'S CREOLE.NGM (Micronesia)
- - - PIJIN.PIS (Solomon Islands)
- - - TOK PISIN.PDG (Papua New Guinea)
- - - TORRES STRAIT CREOLE.TCS (Australia)
- French based (12): AMAPÁ CREOLE.AMD (Brazil)
- - FRENCH GUIANESE.FRE (French Guiana)
- - HAITIAN CREOLE FRENCH.HAT (Haiti)
- - KALDOSH.CKS (New Caledonia)
- - KARIPÚNA CREOLE FRENCH.KMV (Brazil)
- - LESSER ANTILLEAN CREOLE FRENCH.DOM (St. Lucia)
- - LOUISIANA CREOLE FRENCH.LOU (USA)
- - MORISYEN.MFE (Mauritius)
- - REUNION CREOLE FRENCH.RCF (Reunion)
- - SAN MIGUEL CREOLE FRENCH.SME (Panama)
- - SESELWA.CRS (Seychelles)
- - TRINIDAD CREOLE FRENCH.TRF (Trinidad and Tobago)
- German based (1): UNSERDEUTSCH.ULN (Papua New Guinea)
- Kongo based (2): KITUBA.KTU (Zaïre)
- - MUNUKUTUBA.MKW (Congo)
- Malay based (3): BETAWI.BEW (Indonesia, Java, Bali)
- - MALACCAN CREOLE MALAY.CCM (Malaysia, Peninsular)
- - SRI LANKAN CREOLE MALAY.SCI (Sri Lanka)
- Ngbandi based (2): SANGO RIVERAIN.SNJ (Central African Republic)

Creole (66)
- Ngbandi based (2): SANGO.SAJ (Central African Republic)
- Portuguese based (10): CAFUNDO CREOLE.CCD (Brazil)
- - CRIOULO, GULF OF GUINEA.CRI (São Tomé e Príncipe)
- - CRIOULO, UPPER GUINEA.POV (Guinea Bissau)
- - INDO-PORTUGUESE.IDB (Sri Lanka)
- - KORLAI CREOLE PORTUGUESE.VKP (India)
- - MACANESE.MZS (Hong Kong)
- - MALACCAN CREOLE PORTUGUESE.MCM (Malaysia, Peninsular)
- - PAPIAMENTU.PAE (Netherlands Antilles)
- - PIDGIN, TIMOR.TVY (Indonesia, Nusa Tenggara)
- - TERNATEÑO.TMG (Indonesia, Maluku)
- Spanish based (2): CHAVACANO.CBK (Philippines)
- - PALENQUERO.PLN (Colombia)
- Swahili based (1): CUTCHI-SWAHILI.CCL (Kenya)
- Tetun based (1): TETUN DILI.TDT (Indonesia, Nusa Tenggara)

Daic (68)
- Kadai (11)
- - Bu-Rong (2): BUYANG.BYU (China)
- - - YERONG.YRN (China)
- - Lati-Kelao (3): GELAO.KKF (Viet Nam)
- - - LATI, WHITE.LWH (Viet Nam)
- - - LATI.LBT (Viet Nam)
- - Li-Laqua (5): CUN.CUQ (China)
- - - HLAI.LIC (China)
- - - JIAMAO.JIO (China)
- - - LAHA.LHA (Viet Nam)
- - - LAQUA.LAQ (Viet Nam)
- - Unclassified (1): LINGAO.ONB (China)
- Kam-Sui (10): AI-CHAM.AIH (China)
- - CAO MIAO.COV (China)
- - DONG, NORTHERN.DOC (China)
- - DONG, SOUTHERN.KMC (China)
- - LAKA.LBC (China)
- - MAK.MKG (China)
- - MAONAN.MMD (China)
- - MULAM.MLM (China)
- - SUI.SWI (China)
- - T'EN.TCT (China)
- Tai (47)
- - Central (6): E.EEE (China)
- - - MAN CAO LAN.MLC (Viet Nam)
- - - NUNG.NUT (Viet Nam)
- - - TÀY.THO (Viet Nam)
- - - TS'ÜN-LAO.TSL (Viet Nam)
- - - ZHUANG, SOUTHERN.CCY (China)
- - Northern (5): BOUYEI.PCC (China)
- - - NHANG.NHA (Viet Nam)
- - - SAEK.SKB (Laos)
- - - TAI MAEN.TMP (Laos)
- - - ZHUANG, NORTHERN.CCX (China)
- - Southwestern (24)
- - - East Central (20)
- - - - Chiang Saeng (7): PHUAN.PHU (Thailand)
- - - - - SONG.SOA (Thailand)
- - - - - TAI DAENG.TYR (Viet Nam)
- - - - - TAI DAM.BLT (Viet Nam)
- - - - - TAI DÓN.TWH (Viet Nam)
- - - - - TAI, NORTHERN.NOD (Thailand)
- - - - - THAI.THJ (Thailand)
- - - - Lao-Phutai (3): LAO.NOL (Laos)
- - - - - PHU THAI.PHT (Laos)
- - - - - TAI, NORTHEASTERN.TTS (Thailand)
- - - - Northwest (9): AHOM.AHO (India)
- - - - - AITON.AIO (India)
- - - - - KHAMTI.KHT (Myanmar)
- - - - - KHAMYANG.KSU (India)
- - - - - KHÜN.KKH (Myanmar)

Daic (68)
- Tai (47)
- - Southwestern (24)
- - - East Central (20)
- - - - Northwest (9): LÜ.KHB (China)
- - - - - PHAKE.PHK (India)
- - - - - SHAN.SJN (Myanmar)
- - - - - TAI NÜA.TDD (China)
- - - - NYAW.NYW (Thailand)
- - - Southern (1): TAI, SOUTHERN.SOU (Thailand)
- - - TAI HONGJIN.TIZ (China)
- - - TAI YA.CUU (China)
- - - YONG.YNO (Thailand)
- - Unclassified (12): KANG.KYP (Laos)
- - - KUAN.UAN (Laos)
- - - PU KO.PUK (Laos)
- - - RIEN.RIE (Laos)
- - - TAI HANG TONG.THC (Viet Nam)
- - - TAI LONG.THI (Laos)
- - - TAI MAN THANH.TMM (Viet Nam)
- - - TAI PAO.TPO (Laos)
- - - TAY JO.TYJ (Viet Nam)
- - - TAY KHANG.TNU (Laos)
- - - TURUNG.TRY (India)
- - - YOY.YOY (Thailand)

Deaf sign language (104): ADAMOROBE SIGN LANGUAGE.ADS (Ghana)
- ALGERIAN SIGN LANGUAGE.ASP (Algeria)
- AMERICAN SIGN LANGUAGE.ASE (USA)
- ARGENTINE SIGN LANGUAGE.AED (Argentina)
- ARMENIAN SIGN LANGUAGE.AEN (Armenia)
- AUSTRALIAN ABORIGINES SIGN LANGUAGE.ASW (Australia)
- AUSTRALIAN SIGN LANGUAGE.ASF (Australia)
- AUSTRIAN SIGN LANGUAGE.ASQ (Austria)
- BALI SIGN LANGUAGE.BQF (Indonesia, Java, Bali)
- BELGIAN SIGN LANGUAGE.BVS (Belgium)
- BOLIVIAN SIGN LANGUAGE.BVL (Bolivia)
- BRAZILIAN SIGN LANGUAGE.BZS (Brazil)
- BRITISH SIGN LANGUAGE.BHO (United Kingdom)
- BULGARIAN SIGN LANGUAGE.BQN (Bulgaria)
- CANADIAN SIGN LANGUAGE.CSD (Canada)
- CATALONIAN SIGN LANGUAGE.CSC (Spain)
- CHADIAN SIGN LANGUAGE.CDS (Chad)
- CHILEAN SIGN LANGUAGE.CSG (Chile)
- CHINESE SIGN LANGUAGE.CSL (China)
- COLOMBIAN SIGN LANGUAGE.CSN (Colombia)
- COSTA RICAN SIGN LANGUAGE.CSR (Costa Rica)
- CZECH SIGN LANGUAGE.CSE (Czech Republic)
- DANISH SIGN LANGUAGE.DSL (Denmark)
- DUTCH SIGN LANGUAGE.DSE (Netherlands)
- ECUADORIAN SIGN LANGUAGE.ECS (Ecuador)
- EL SALVADORAN SIGN LANGUAGE.ESN (El Salvador)
- ESKIMO SIGN LANGUAGE.ESL (Canada)
- ETHIOPIAN SIGN LANGUAGE.ETH (Ethiopia)
- FINNISH SIGN LANGUAGE.FSE (Finland)
- FRENCH CANADIAN SIGN LANGUAGE.FCS (Canada)
- FRENCH SIGN LANGUAGE.FSL (France)
- GERMAN SIGN LANGUAGE.GSG (Germany)
- GHANAIAN SIGN LANGUAGE.GSE (Ghana)
- GREEK SIGN LANGUAGE.GSS (Greece)
- GUATEMALAN SIGN LANGUAGE.GSM (Guatemala)
- HAWAI'I PIDGIN SIGN LANGUAGE.HPS (USA)
- ICELANDIC SIGN LANGUAGE.ICL (Iceland)
- INDIAN SIGN LANGUAGE.INS (India)
- INDONESIAN SIGN LANGUAGE.INL (Indonesia, Java, Bali)
- IRISH SIGN LANGUAGE.ISG (Ireland)
- ISRAELI SIGN LANGUAGE.ISL (Israel)
- ITALIAN SIGN LANGUAGE.ISE (Italy)

Deaf sign language (104): JAMAICAN COUNTRY SIGN LANGUAGE.JCS (Jamaica)
- JAPANESE SIGN LANGUAGE.JSL (Japan)
- JORDANIAN SIGN LANGUAGE.JOS (Jordan)
- KENYAN SIGN LANGUAGE.XKI (Kenya)
- KOREAN SIGN LANGUAGE.KVK (Korea, South)
- KUALA LUMPUR SIGN LANGUAGE.KGI (Malaysia, Peninsular)
- LATVIAN SIGN LANGUAGE.LSL (Latvia)
- LIBYAN SIGN LANGUAGE.LBS (Libya)
- LITHUANIAN SIGN LANGUAGE.LLS (Lithuania)
- LYONS SIGN LANGUAGE.LSG (France)
- MALAYSIAN SIGN LANGUAGE.XML (Malaysia, Peninsular)
- MALTESE SIGN LANGUAGE.MDL (Malta)
- MARTHA'S VINEYARD SIGN LANGUAGE.MRE (USA)
- MAYAN SIGN LANGUAGE.MSD (Mexico)
- MEXICAN SIGN LANGUAGE.MFS (Mexico)
- MONGOLIAN SIGN LANGUAGE.QMM (Mongolian Peoples Republic)
- MOROCCAN SIGN LANGUAGE.XMS (Morocco)
- NAMIBIAN SIGN LANGUAGE.NBS (Namibia)
- NEPALESE SIGN LANGUAGE.NSP (Nepal)
- NEW ZEALAND SIGN LANGUAGE.NZS (New Zealand)
- NICARAGUAN SIGN LANGUAGE.NCS (Nicaragua)
- NIGERIAN SIGN LANGUAGE.NSI (Nigeria)
- NORWEGIAN SIGN LANGUAGE.NSL (Norway)
- NOVA SCOTIAN SIGN LANGUAGE.NSR (Canada)
- OLD KENTISH SIGN LANGUAGE.OKL (United Kingdom)
- PAKISTAN SIGN LANGUAGE.PKS (Pakistan)
- PENANG SIGN LANGUAGE.PSG (Malaysia, Peninsular)
- PERSIAN SIGN LANGUAGE.PSC (Iran)
- PERUVIAN SIGN LANGUAGE.PRL (Peru)
- PHILIPPINE SIGN LANGUAGE.PSP (Philippines)
- POLISH SIGN LANGUAGE.PSO (Poland)
- PORTUGUESE SIGN LANGUAGE.PSR (Portugal)
- PROVIDENCIA SIGN LANGUAGE.PRO (Colombia)
- PUERTO RICAN SIGN LANGUAGE.PSL (Puerto Rico)
- RENNELLESE SIGN LANGUAGE.RSI (Solomon Islands)
- ROMANIAN SIGN LANGUAGE.RMS (Romania)
- RUSSIAN SIGN LANGUAGE.RSL (Russia, Europe)
- SAUDI ARABIAN SIGN LANGUAGE.SDL (Saudi Arabia)
- SCANDINAVIAN PIDGIN SIGN LANGUAGE.SPF (Sweden)
- SINGAPORE SIGN LANGUAGE.SLS (Singapore)
- SLOVAKIAN SIGN LANGUAGE.SVK (Slovakia)
- SOUTH AFRICAN SIGN LANGUAGE.SFS (South Africa)
- SPANISH SIGN LANGUAGE.SSP (Spain)
- SRI LANKAN SIGN LANGUAGE.SQS (Sri Lanka)
- SWEDISH SIGN LANGUAGE.SWL (Sweden)
- SWISS-FRENCH SIGN LANGUAGE.SSR (Switzerland)
- SWISS-GERMAN SIGN LANGUAGE.SGG (Switzerland)
- SWISS-ITALIAN SIGN LANGUAGE.SLF (Switzerland)
- TAIWANESE SIGN LANGUAGE.TSS (Taiwan)
- TANZANIAN SIGN LANGUAGE.TZA (Tanzania)
- THAI SIGN LANGUAGE.TSQ (Thailand)
- TUNISIAN SIGN LANGUAGE.TSE (Tunisia)
- TURKISH SIGN LANGUAGE.TSM (Turkey)
- UGANDAN SIGN LANGUAGE.UGN (Uganda)
- UKRAINIAN SIGN LANGUAGE.UKL (Ukraine)
- URUBÚ-KAAPOR SIGN LANGUAGE.UKS (Brazil)
- URUGUAYAN SIGN LANGUAGE.UGY (Uruguay)
- VENEZUELAN SIGN LANGUAGE.VSL (Venezuela)
- YIDDISH SIGN LANGUAGE.YDS (Israel)
- YUGOSLAVIAN SIGN LANGUAGE.YSL (Yugoslavia)
- ZAMBIAN SIGN LANGUAGE.ZSL (Zambia)
- ZIMBABWE SIGN LANGUAGE.ZIB (Zimbabwe)

Dravidian (78)
- Central (5)
- - Kolami-Naiki (2): KOLAMI, NORTHWESTERN.KFB (India)
- - - KOLAMI, SOUTHEASTERN.NIT (India)
- - Parji-Gadaba (3): DURUWA.PCI (India)
- - - GADABA.GDB (India)
- - - OLLARI.OLL (India)
- Northern (5): BRAHUI.BRH (Pakistan)
- - KUMARBHAG PAHARIA.KMJ (India)
- - KURUX, NEPALI.KXL (Nepal)
- - KURUX.KVN (India)
- - SAURIA PAHARIA.MJT (India)
- South-Central (24)
- - Gondi-Kui (19)
- - - Gondi (11): ABUJMARIA.ABJ (India)
- - - - GONDI, NORTHERN.GON (India)
- - - - GONDI, SOUTHERN.GGO (India)
- - - - KHIRWAR.KWX (India)
- - - - MARIA, DANDAMI.DAQ (India)
- - - - MARIA.MRR (India)
- - - - MURIA, EASTERN.EMU (India)
- - - - MURIA, FAR WESTERN.FMU (India)
- - - - MURIA, WESTERN.MUT (India)
- - - - NAGARCHAL.NBG (India)
- - - - PARDHAN.PCH (India)
- - - Konda-Kui (8)
- - - - Konda (2): KONDA-DORA.KFC (India)
- - - - - NUKA-DORA.NUK (India)
- - - - Manda-Kui (6)
- - - - - Kui-Kuvi (4): JATAPU.JTP (India)
- - - - - - KOYA.KFF (India)
- - - - - - KUI.KXU (India)
- - - - - - KUVI.KXV (India)
- - - - - Manda-Pengo (2): MANDA.MHA (India)
- - - - - - PENGO.PEG (India)
- - Telugu (5): CHENCHU.CDE (India)
- - - SAVARA.SVR (India)
- - - TELUGU.TCW (India)
- - - WADDAR.WBQ (India)
- - - YANADI.YBF (India)
- Southern (28)
- - Tamil-Kannada (23)
- - - Kannada (4): BADAGA.BFQ (India)
- - - - HOLIYA.HOY (India)
- - - - KANNADA.KJV (India)
- - - - URALI.URL (India)
- - - Tamil-Kodagu (19)
- - - - Kodagu (6): ALU.AUX (India)
- - - - - KANNADA, SOUTHERN.SKJ (India)
- - - - - KODAGU.KFA (India)
- - - - - KURUMBA, ALU.QKA (India)
- - - - - KURUMBA, JENNU.QKJ (India)
- - - - - KURUMBA.KFI (India)
- - - - Tamil-Malayalam (11)
- - - - - Malayalam (5): KADAR.KEJ (India)
- - - - - - MALAYALAM.MJS (India)
- - - - - - PALIYAN.PCF (India)
- - - - - - PANIYA.PCG (India)
- - - - - - YERAVA.YEA (India)
- - - - - Tamil (6): IRULA.IRU (India)
- - - - - - KAIKADI.KEP (India)
- - - - - - KURUMBA, BETTA.QKB (India)
- - - - - - MANNAN.MJV (India)
- - - - - - SHOLAGA.SLE (India)
- - - - - - TAMIL.TCV (India)
- - - - Toda-Kota (2): KOTA.KFE (India)
- - - - - TODA.TCX (India)
- - Tulu (4)
- - - Koraga (2): KORAGA, KORRA.KFD (India)

Dravidian (78)
- Southern (28)
- - Tulu (4)
- - - Koraga (2): KORAGA, MUDU.VMD (India)
- - - BELLARI.BRW (India)
- - - TULU.TCY (India)
- - Unclassified (1): ULLATAN.ULL (India)
- Unclassified (16): ADIYAN.ADN (India)
- - ALLAR.ALL (India)
- - ARANADAN.AAF (India)
- - BAZIGAR.BFR (India)
- - BHARIA.BHA (India)
- - KAMAR.KEQ (India)
- - KANIKKARAN.KEV (India)
- - KUDIYA.KFG (India)
- - KURICHIYA.KFH (India)
- - MALANKURAVAN.MJO (India)
- - MALAPANDARAM.MJP (India)
- - MALARYAN.MJQ (India)
- - MALAVEDAN.MJR (India)
- - MANNA-DORA.MJU (India)
- - MUTHUVAN.MUV (India)
- - VISHAVAN.VIS (India)

East Bird's Head (3)
- Meax (2): MEYAH.MEJ (Indonesia, Irian Jaya)
- - MOSKONA.MTJ (Indonesia, Irian Jaya)
- MANIKION.MNX (Indonesia, Irian Jaya)

East Papuan (36)
- Bougainville (13)
- - East (9)
- - - Buin (3): BUIN.BUO (Papua New Guinea)
- - - - SIWAI.SIW (Papua New Guinea)
- - - - UISAI.UIS (Papua New Guinea)
- - - Nasioi (6): KOROMIRA.KQJ (Papua New Guinea)
- - - - LANTANAI.LNI (Papua New Guinea)
- - - - NAASIOI.NAS (Papua New Guinea)
- - - - NAGOVISI.NCO (Papua New Guinea)
- - - - OUNE.OUE (Papua New Guinea)
- - - - SIMEKU.SMZ (Papua New Guinea)
- - West (4)
- - - Keriaka (1): KERIAKA.KJX (Papua New Guinea)
- - - Rotokas (2): EIVO.EIV (Papua New Guinea)
- - - - ROTOKAS.ROO (Papua New Guinea)
- - - KUNUA.KYX (Papua New Guinea)
- Reef Islands-Santa Cruz (3): AYIWO.NFL (Solomon Islands)
- - NANGGU.NAN (Solomon Islands)
- - SANTA CRUZ.STC (Solomon Islands)
- Yele-Solomons-New Britain (20)
- - New Britain (12)
- - - Anem (1): ANEM.ANZ (Papua New Guinea)
- - - Baining-Taulil (7): KAIRAK.CKR (Papua New Guinea)
- - - - MAKOLKOL.ZMH (Papua New Guinea)
- - - - MALI.GCC (Papua New Guinea)
- - - - QAQET.BYX (Papua New Guinea)
- - - - SIMBALI.SMG (Papua New Guinea)
- - - - TAULIL-BUTAM.TUH (Papua New Guinea)
- - - - URA.URO (Papua New Guinea)
- - - Kuot (1): KUOT.KTO (Papua New Guinea)
- - - Sulka (1): SULKA.SLK (Papua New Guinea)
- - - Wasi (1): PELE-ATA.ATA (Papua New Guinea)
- - - KOL.KOL (Papua New Guinea)
- - Yele-Solomons (8)
- - - Central Solomons (4): BANIATA.BNT (Solomon Islands)
- - - - BILUA.BLB (Solomon Islands)
- - - - LAVUKALEVE.LVK (Solomon Islands)
- - - - SAVO.SVS (Solomon Islands)
- - - Kazukuru (3): DORORO.DRR (Solomon Islands)

East Papuan (36)
- Yele-Solomons-New Britain (20)
- - Yele-Solomons (8)
- - - Kazukuru (3): GULIGULI.GLG (Solomon Islands)
- - - - KAZUKURU.KZK (Solomon Islands)
- - - Yele (1): YELE.YLE (Papua New Guinea)

English-Tahitian cant (1): PITCAIRN-NORFOLK.PIH (Norfolk Island)

Eskimo-Aleut (11)
- Aleut (1): ALEUT.ALW (USA)
- Eskimo (10)
- - Inuit (5): INUKTITUT, EASTERN CANADIAN.ESB (Canada)
- - - INUKTITUT, GREENLANDIC.ESG (Greenland)
- - - INUKTITUT, NORTH ALASKAN.ESI (USA)
- - - INUKTITUT, NORTHWEST ALASKA INUPIAT.ESK (USA)
- - - INUKTITUT, WESTERN CANADIAN.ESC (Canada)
- - Yupik (5)
- - - Alaskan (2): YUPIK, CENTRAL.ESU (USA)
- - - - YUPIK, PACIFIC GULF.EMS (USA)
- - - Siberian (3): YUPIK, CENTRAL SIBERIAN.ESS (USA)
- - - - YUPIK, NAUKAN.YNK (Russia, Asia)
- - - - YUPIK, SIRENIK.YSR (Russia, Asia)

Geelvink Bay (34)
- East Geelvink Bay (11): BAPU.BPO (Indonesia, Irian Jaya)
- - BARAPASI.BRP (Indonesia, Irian Jaya)
- - BAUZI.PAU (Indonesia, Irian Jaya)
- - BURATE.BTI (Indonesia, Irian Jaya)
- - DEMISA.DEI (Indonesia, Irian Jaya)
- - KOFEI.KPI (Indonesia, Irian Jaya)
- - NISA.NIC (Indonesia, Irian Jaya)
- - SAURI.SAH (Indonesia, Irian Jaya)
- - TEFARO.TFO (Indonesia, Irian Jaya)
- - TUNGGARE.TRT (Indonesia, Irian Jaya)
- - WORIA.WOR (Indonesia, Irian Jaya)
- Lakes Plain (20)
- - Awera (1): AWERA.AWR (Indonesia, Irian Jaya)
- - East Lakes Plain (3): DABRA.DBA (Indonesia, Irian Jaya)
- - - FOAU.FLH (Indonesia, Irian Jaya)
- - - TAWORTA.TBP (Indonesia, Irian Jaya)
- - Rasawa-Saponi (2): RASAWA.RAC (Indonesia, Irian Jaya)
- - - SAPONI.SPI (Indonesia, Irian Jaya)
- - Tariku (14)
- - - Central (2): EDOPI.DBF (Indonesia, Irian Jaya)
- - - - IAU.TMU (Indonesia, Irian Jaya)
- - - Duvle (1): DUVLE.DUV (Indonesia, Irian Jaya)
- - - East (8): BIRITAI.BQQ (Indonesia, Irian Jaya)
- - - - DOUTAI.TDS (Indonesia, Irian Jaya)
- - - - ERITAI.BAD (Indonesia, Irian Jaya)
- - - - KAIY.TCQ (Indonesia, Irian Jaya)
- - - - KWERISA.KKB (Indonesia, Irian Jaya)
- - - - PAPASENA.PAS (Indonesia, Irian Jaya)
- - - - SIKARITAI.TTY (Indonesia, Irian Jaya)
- - - - WARI.WBE (Indonesia, Irian Jaya)
- - - West (3): FAYU.FAU (Indonesia, Irian Jaya)
- - - - KIRIKIRI.KIY (Indonesia, Irian Jaya)
- - - - TAUSE.TAD (Indonesia, Irian Jaya)
- Northern (1)
- - Lakes Plain (1)
- - - Tariku (1)
- - - - East (1): OBOKUITAI.AFZ (Indonesia, Irian Jaya)
- Yawa (1): YAWA.YVA (Indonesia, Irian Jaya)
- SAWERU.SWR (Indonesia, Irian Jaya)

Gulf (4): ATAKAPA.ALE (USA)
- CHITIMACHA.CHM (USA)
- NATCHEZ.NCZ (USA)
- TUNICA.TUK (USA)

Hmong-Mien (32)
- Hmongic (26)
- - Bunu (5): BUNU, BAHENG.PHA (China)
- - - BUNU, BU-NAO.BWX (China)
- - - BUNU, JIONGNAI.PNU (China)
- - - BUNU, WUNAI.BWN (China)
- - - BUNU, YOUNUO.BUH (China)
- - Chuanqiandian (16): HMONG DAW.MWW (China)
- - - HMONG NJUA.BLU (China)
- - - HMONG, CENTRAL HUISHUI.HMC (China)
- - - HMONG, CENTRAL MASHAN.HMM (China)
- - - HMONG, CHONGANJIANG.HMJ (China)
- - - HMONG, EASTERN HUISHUI.HME (China)
- - - HMONG, LUOPOHE.HML (China)
- - - HMONG, NORTHEASTERN DIAN.HMD (China)
- - - HMONG, NORTHERN GUIYANG.HUJ (China)
- - - HMONG, NORTHERN HUISHUI.HMN (China)
- - - HMONG, NORTHERN MASHAN.HMO (China)
- - - HMONG, SOUTHERN GUIYANG.HMY (China)
- - - HMONG, SOUTHERN MASHAN.HMA (China)
- - - HMONG, SOUTHWESTERN GUIYANG.HMG (China)
- - - HMONG, SOUTHWESTERN HUISHUI.HMH (China)
- - - HMONG, WESTERN MASHAN.HMW (China)
- - Qiandong (3): HMONG, EASTERN QIANDONG.HMQ (China)
- - - HMONG, NORTHERN QIANDONG.HEA (China)
- - - HMONG, SOUTHERN QIANDONG.HMS (China)
- - Xiangxi (2): HMONG, EASTERN XIANGXI.MUQ (China)
- - - HMONG, WESTERN XIANGXI.MMR (China)
- Mienic (5)
- - Biao-Jiao (1): BIAO-JIAO MIEN.BJE (China)
- - Mian-Jin (3): BIAO MIEN.BMT (China)
- - - IU MIEN.IUM (China)
- - - KIM MUN.MJI (China)
- - Zaomin (1): BA PAI.BPN (China)
- Ho Nte (1): SHE.SHX (China)

Hokan (27)
- Esselen-Yuman (9)
- - Yuman (9)
- - - Cochimi (1): COCHIMÍ.COJ (Mexico)
- - - Delta-Californian (2): COCOPA.COC (Mexico)
- - - - KUMIÁI.DIH (Mexico)
- - - Kiliwa (1): KILIWI.KLB (Mexico)
- - - Pai (1): PAIPAI.PPI (Mexico)
- - - River Yuman (3): MARICOPA.MRC (USA)
- - - - MOHAVE.MOV (USA)
- - - - QUECHAN.YUM (USA)
- - - Upland Yuman (1): HAVASUPAI-WALAPAI-YAVAPAI.YUF (USA)
- Northern (12)
- - Karok-Shasta (4)
- - - Shasta-Palaihninan (3)
- - - - Palaihninan (2): ACHUMAWI.ACH (USA)
- - - - - ATSUGEWI.ATW (USA)
- - - - Shastan (1): SHASTA.SHT (USA)
- - - KAROK.KYH (USA)
- - Pomo (7)
- - - Russian River and Eastern (6)
- - - - Eastern (1): POMO, EASTERN.PEB (USA)
- - - - Russian River (5)
- - - - - Northeastern (1): POMO, NORTHEASTERN.PEF (USA)
- - - - - Northern (1): POMO, NORTHERN.PEJ (USA)
- - - - - Southern (3): KASHAYA.KJU (USA)
- - - - - - POMO, CENTRAL.POO (USA)
- - - - - - POMO, SOUTHERN.PEQ (USA)

Hokan (27)
- Northern (12)
- - Pomo (7)
- - - Southeastern (1): POMO, SOUTHEASTERN.PEO (USA)
- - Yana (1): YANA.YNN (USA)
- Salinan-Seri (3): CHUMASH.CHS (USA)
- - SALINAN.SAL (USA)
- - SERI.SEI (Mexico)
- Tequistlatecan (2): CHONTAL OF OAXACA, HIGHLAND.CHD (Mexico)
- - CHONTAL OF OAXACA, LOWLAND.CLO (Mexico)
- Washo (1): WASHO.WAS (USA)

Huavean (4): HUAVE, SAN DIONISIO DEL MAR.HVE (Mexico)
- HUAVE, SAN FRANCISCO DEL MAR.HUE (Mexico)
- HUAVE, SAN MATEO DEL MAR.HUV (Mexico)
- HUAVE, SANTA MARÍA DEL MAR.HVV (Mexico)

Indo-European (425)
- Albanian (4)
- - Gheg (1): ALBANIAN, GHEG.ALS (Yugoslavia)
- - Tosk (3): ALBANIAN, ARBËRESHË.AAE (Italy)
- - - ALBANIAN, ARVANITIKA.AAT (Greece)
- - - ALBANIAN, TOSK.ALN (Albania)
- Armenian (2): ARMENIAN.ARM (Armenia)
- - LOMAVREN.RMI (Armenia)
- Baltic (2): LATVIAN.LAT (Latvia)
- - LITHUANIAN.LIT (Lithuania)
- Celtic (7)
- - Insular (7)
- - - Brythonic (3): BRETON.BRT (France)
- - - - CORNISH.CRN (United Kingdom)
- - - - WELSH.WLS (United Kingdom)
- - - Goidelic (4): GAELIC, IRISH.GLI (Ireland)
- - - - GAELIC, SCOTS.GLS (United Kingdom)
- - - - MANX.MJD (United Kingdom)
- - - - SHELTA.STH (Ireland)
- Germanic (37)
- - East (1): GOTHIC.GOF (Ukraine)
- - North (10)
- - - East Scandinavian (5): DANISH.DNS (Denmark)
- - - - JUTISH.JUT (Denmark)
- - - - SWEDISH.SWD (Sweden)
- - - - TRAVELLER DANISH.RMD (Denmark)
- - - - TRAVELLER SWEDISH.RMU (Sweden)
- - - Transitional Scandinavian (1): NORWEGIAN, BOKMAL.NRR (Norway)
- - - West Scandinavian (4): FAROESE.FAE (Denmark)
- - - - ICELANDIC.ICE (Iceland)
- - - - NORWEGIAN, NYNORSK.NRN (Norway)
- - - - TRAVELLER NORWEGIAN.RMG (Norway)
- - West (26)
- - - Continental (20)
- - - - High (15): BAVARIAN.BAR (Austria)
- - - - - CIMBRIAN.CIM (Italy)
- - - - - FRANKISH.FRK (Germany)
- - - - - GERMAN, COLONIA TOVAR.GCT (Venezuela)
- - - - - GERMAN, HUTTERITE.GEH (Canada)
- - - - - GERMAN, PENNSYLVANIA.PDC (USA)
- - - - - GERMAN, STANDARD.GER (Germany)
- - - - - LUXEMBOURGEOIS.LUX (Luxembourg)
- - - - - MAINFRÄNKISCH.VMF (Germany)
- - - - - MÓCHENO.QMO (Italy)
- - - - - SCHWYZERDÜTSCH.GSW (Switzerland)
- - - - - SWABIAN.SWG (Germany)
- - - - - WALSER.WAE (Italy)
- - - - - YENICHE.YEC (Germany)
- - - - - YIDDISH.YDD (Israel)
- - - - Low (5)
- - - - - Dutch (2): AFRIKAANS.AFK (South Africa)
- - - - - - DUTCH.DUT (Netherlands)

Indo-European (425)
- Indo-Iranian (302)
- - Indo-Aryan (219)
- - - Northwestern zone (40)
- - - - Dardic (28)
- - - - - Shina (7): SHINA.SCL (Pakistan)
- - - - - - USHOJO.USH (Pakistan)
- - - - Lahnda (7): BAHAWALPURI.BGB (India)
- - - - - HINDKO, NORTHERN.HNO (Pakistan)
- - - - - HINDKO, SOUTHERN.HIN (Pakistan)
- - - - - KHETRANI.QKT (Pakistan)
- - - - - PANJABI, MIRPUR.PMU (India)
- - - - - PANJABI, WESTERN.PNB (Pakistan)
- - - - - SARAIKI.SKR (Pakistan)
- - - - Sindhi (5): JADGALI.JAV (Pakistan)
- - - - - KACHCHI.KFR (India)
- - - - - LASI.LSS (Pakistan)
- - - - - SINDHI BHIL.SBN (Pakistan)
- - - - - SINDHI.SND (Pakistan)
- - - Nuristani (6): ASHKUN.ASK (Afghanistan)
- - - - KAMVIRI.QMV (Afghanistan)
- - - - KATI.BSH (Afghanistan)
- - - - PRASUNI.PRN (Afghanistan)
- - - - TREGAMI.TRM (Afghanistan)
- - - - WAIGALI.WBK (Afghanistan)
- - - - Sinhalese-Maldivian (3): MALDIVIAN.SNM (Maldives)
- - - - SINHALA.SNH (Sri Lanka)
- - - - VEDDAH.VED (Sri Lanka)
- - - Southern zone (16)
- - - - Konkani (10): KATKARI.KFU (India)
- - - - - KONKANI, GOANESE.GOM (India)
- - - - - KONKANI.KNK (India)
- - - - - KUKNA.KEX (India)
- - - - - MANGELAS.MVL (India)
- - - - - PHUDAGI.PHD (India)
- - - - - SAMVEDI.SMV (India)
- - - - - THAKURI.THK (India)
- - - - - VADVAL.VAD (India)
- - - - - VARLI.VAV (India)
- - - - Unclassified (5): ARE.AAG (India)
- - - - - BHALAY.BHX (India)
- - - - - DECCAN.DCC (India)
- - - - - GOWLAN.GOJ (India)
- - - - - VARHADI-NAGPURI.VAH (India)
- - - Southern zone
- - - - (1): IKRANI.IKR (India)
- - - Southern zone (16): MARATHI.MRT (India)
- - - Unclassified (13): CHIK-BARIK.CKB (India)
- - - - DARAI.DRY (Nepal)
- - - - DHANWAR.DHW (Nepal)
- - - - KANJARI.KFT (India)
- - - - KUMHALI.KRA (Nepal)
- - - - MINA.MYI (India)
- - - - OD.ODK (Pakistan)
- - - - PALI.PLL (India)
- - - - RELI.REI (India)
- - - - TIPPERA.TPE (Bangladesh)
- - - - USUI.USI (Bangladesh)
- - - - VAAGRI BOOLI.VAA (India)
- - - - VAGHRI.VGR (Pakistan)
- - - SANSKRIT.SKT (India)
- - Iranian (81)
- - - Eastern (14)
- - - - Northeastern (2): OSETIN.OSE (Georgia)
- - - - - YAGNOBI.YAI (Tajikistan)
- - - - Southeastern (12)
- - - - - Pamir (7)
- - - - - - Shugni-Yazgulami (3): SARIKOLI.SRH (China)
- - - - - - - SHUGHNI.SGH (Tajikistan)

Indo-European (425)
- Italic (47)
- - Romance (46)
- - - Italo-Western (37)
- - - - Western (28)
- - - - - Ibero-Romance (19)
- - - - - - North (18)
- - - - - - - Western (3): FALA.FAX (Spain)
- - - - - - - - GALICIAN.GLN (Spain)
- - - - - - - - - PORTUGUESE.POR (Portugal)
- - - - - - South (1): MOZARABIC.MXI (Spain)
- - - Southern (5)
- - - - Corsican (1): CORSICAN.COI (France)
- - - - Sardinian (4): SARDINIAN, CAMPIDANESE.SRO (Italy)
- - - - - SARDINIAN, GALLURESE.SDN (Italy)
- - - - - SARDINIAN, LOGUDORESE.SRD (Italy)
- - - - - SARDINIAN, SASSARESE.SDC (Italy)
- Slavic (18)
- - East (4): BELORUSSIAN.RUW (Belarus)
- - - RUSSIAN.RUS (Russia, Europe)
- - - RUSYN.RUE (Ukraine)
- - - UKRAINIAN.UKR (Ukraine)
- - South (6)
- - - Eastern (3): BULGARIAN.BLG (Bulgaria)
- - - - MACEDONIAN.MKJ (Macedonia)
- - - - SLAVONIC, OLD CHURCH.SLN (Russia, Europe)
- - - Western (3): ROMANO-SERBIAN.RSB (Yugoslavia)
- - - - SERBO-CROATIAN.SRC (Yugoslavia)
- - - - SLOVENIAN.SLV (Slovenia)
- - West (8)
- - - Czech-Slovak (3): CZECH.CZC (Czech Republic)
- - - - KNAANIC.CZK (Czech Republic)
- - - - SLOVAK.SLO (Slovakia)
- - - Lechitic (3): KASHUBIAN.CSB (Poland)
- - - - POLABIAN.POX (Germany)
- - - - POLISH.PQL (Poland)
- - - Sorbian (2): SORBIAN, LOWER.WEE (Germany)
- - - - SORBIAN, UPPER.WEN (Germany)

Iroquoian (9)
- Northern Iroquoian (8)
- - Five Nations (5)
- - - Mohawk-Oneida (2): MOHAWK.MOH (Canada)
- - - - ONEIDA.ONE (Canada)
- - - Seneca-Onondaga (3)
- - - - Onondaga (1): ONONDAGA.ONO (Canada)
- - - - Seneca-Cayuga (2): CAYUGA.CAY (Canada)
- - - - - SENECA.SEE (USA)
- - Huron (1): WYANDOT.WYA (USA)
- - Tuscarora-Nottoway (1): TUSCARORA.TUS (Canada)
- - LAURENTIAN.LRE (Canada)
- Southern Iroquoian (1)
- - Cherokee (1): CHEROKEE.CER (USA)

Japanese (12)
- Japanese (1): JAPANESE.JPN (Japan)
- Ryukyuan (11)
- - Amami-Okinawan (8)
- - - Northern Amami-Okinawan (4): AMAMI-OSHIMA, NORTHERN.RYN (Japan)
- - - - AMAMI-OSHIMA, SOUTHERN.AMS (Japan)
- - - - KIKAI.KZG (Japan)
- - - - TOKU-NO-SHIMA.TKN (Japan)
- - - Southern Amami-Okinawan (4): KUNIGAMI.XUG (Japan)
- - - - OKI-NO-ERABU.OKN (Japan)
- - - - OKINAWAN, CENTRAL.RYU (Japan)
- - - - YORON.YOX (Japan)
- - Sakishima (3): MIYAKO.MVI (Japan)
- - - YAEYAMA.RYS (Japan)
- - - YONAGUNI.YOI (Japan)

Jivaroan (5)
- Candoshi (1): CANDOSHI-SHAPRA.CBU (Peru)
- Shuar (4): ACHUAR-SHIWIAR.ACU (Peru)
- - AGUARUNA.AGR (Peru)
- - HUAMBISA.HUB (Peru)
- - SHUAR.JIV (Ecuador)

Katukinan (3): KANAMARÍ.KNM (Brazil)
- KATAWIXI.QKI (Brazil)
- KATUKÍNA.KAV (Brazil)

Keres (2): KERES, EASTERN.KEE (USA)
- KERES, WESTERN.KJQ (USA)

Khoisan (35)
- Hatsa (1): HATSA.HTS (Tanzania)
- Sandawe (1): SANDAWE.SBR (Tanzania)
- Southern Africa (33)
- - Central (20)
- - - Hain//um (1): HAI//OM.HGM (Namibia)
- - - Kwadi (1): KWADI.KWZ (Angola)
- - - Nama (3): KORANA.KQZ (South Africa)
- - - - NAMA.NAQ (Namibia)
- - - - XIRI.XII (South Africa)
- - - Tshu-Khwe (15)
- - - - Central (1): DETI-KHWE.DET (Botswana)
- - - - North Central (2): GANÁDE.GNE (Botswana)
- - - - - SHUA.SHG (Botswana)
- - - - Northeast (5): GABAKE-NTSHORI.GZZ (Botswana)
- - - - - HIECHWARE.HIE (Botswana)
- - - - - HIOTSHUWAU.HIO (Botswana)
- - - - - KOSSEE.KSO (Botswana)
- - - - - KWE-ETSHORI.KWQ (Botswana)
- - - - Northwest (4): BUKA-KHWE.BUZ (Botswana)
- - - - - GANA-KHWE.GNK (Botswana)
- - - - - HANDÁ.HNH (Botswana)
- - - - - XUN.XUU (Angola)
- - - - Southwest (3): GANI-KHWE.GNX (Botswana)
- - - - - GWI-KHWE.GWJ (Botswana)
- - - - - NARO.NHR (Botswana)
- - Northern (7): !O!UNG.OUN (Angola)
- - - 'AKHOE.AKE (Namibia)
- - - KUNG-EKOKA.KNW (Namibia)
- - - KUNG-GOBABIS.AUE (Namibia)
- - - KUNG-TSUMKWE.KTZ (Namibia)
- - - MALIGO.MWJ (Angola)
- - - VASEKELA BUSHMAN.VAJ (Namibia)
- - Southern (6)
- - - !Kwi (4): //XEGWI.XEG (South Africa)
- - - - /XAM.XAM (South Africa)
- - - - NG'HUKI.NGH (South Africa)
- - - - SEROA.KQU (South Africa)
- - - Hua (2): !XOO.NMN (Botswana)
- - - - =HUA.HUC (Botswana)

Kiowa Tanoan (5)
- Kiowa-Towa (2)
- - Kiowa (1): KIOWA.KIO (USA)
- - Towa (1): JEMEZ.TOW (USA)
- Tewa-Tiwa (3)
- - Tewa (1): TEWA.TEW (USA)
- - Tiwa (2): TIWA, NORTHERN.TAO (USA)
- - - TIWA, SOUTHERN.TIX (USA)

Kwomtari-Baibai (6)
- Baibai (2): BAIBAI.BBF (Papua New Guinea)
- - NAI.BIO (Papua New Guinea)
- Kwomtari (3): FAS.FAS (Papua New Guinea)
- - GURIASO.GRX (Papua New Guinea)
- - KWOMTARI.KWO (Papua New Guinea)
- Pyu (1): PYU.PBY (Papua New Guinea)

Language Isolate (31): AINU.AIN (Japan)
- ANDOQUE.ANO (Colombia)
- BURMESO.BZU (Indonesia, Irian Jaya)
- BURUSHASKI.BSK (Pakistan)
- BUSA.BHF (Papua New Guinea)
- CAMSÁ.KBH (Colombia)
- CAYUBABA.CAT (Bolivia)
- GILYAK.NIV (Russia, Asia)
- ITONAMA.ITO (Bolivia)
- KARKAR-YURI.YUJ (Papua New Guinea)
- KIBIRI.PRM (Papua New Guinea)
- KOREAN.KKN (Korea, South)
- KUTENAI.KUN (Canada)
- MBUGU.MHD (Tanzania)
- NIHALI.NHL (India)
- PANKARARÚ.PAZ (Brazil)
- PAUWI.PKA (Indonesia, Irian Jaya)
- PUELCHE.PUE (Argentina)
- PUINAVE.PUI (Colombia)
- PURÉPECHA.TSZ (Mexico)
- TICUNA.TCA (Peru)
- TOL.JIC (Honduras)
- TRUMAÍ.TPY (Brazil)
- TUXÁ.TUD (Brazil)
- WARAO.WBA (Venezuela)
- WAREMBORI.WSA (Indonesia, Irian Jaya)
- YÁMANA.YAG (Chile)
- YALE.NCE (Papua New Guinea)
- YUCHI.YUC (USA)
- YURACARE.YUE (Bolivia)
- ZUNI.ZUN (USA)

Left May (7): AMA.AMM (Papua New Guinea)
- BO.BPW (Papua New Guinea)
- ITERI.ITR (Papua New Guinea)
- NAKWI.NAX (Papua New Guinea)
- NIMO.NIW (Papua New Guinea)
- OWINIGA.OWI (Papua New Guinea)
- ROCKY PEAK.ROK (Papua New Guinea)

Lule-Vilela (1): VILELA.VIL (Argentina)

Macro-Ge (32)
- Bororo (3)
- - Bororo Proper (2): BORÔRO.BOR (Brazil)
- - - UMOTÍNA.UMO (Brazil)
- - Otuke (1): OTUKE.OTU (Brazil)
- Botocudo (1): KRENAK.KQQ (Brazil)
- Chiquito (1): CHIQUITANO.CAX (Bolivia)
- Fulnio (1): FULNIÔ.FUN (Brazil)
- Ge-Kaingang (16)
- - Ge (13)
- - - Central (4)
- - - - Acua (3): XAKRIABÁ.XKR (Brazil)
- - - - - XAVÁNTE.XAV (Brazil)
- - - - - XERÉNTE.XER (Brazil)
- - - - ACROÁ.ACS (Brazil)
- - - Northwest (9)
- - - - Apinaye (1): APINAYÉ.APN (Brazil)
- - - - Kayapo (1): KAYAPÓ.TXU (Brazil)
- - - - Kreen-Akarore (1): KREEN-AKARORE.KRE (Brazil)

Macro-Ge (32)
- Ge-Kaingang (16)
- - Ge (13)
- - - Northwest (9)
- - - - Suya (1): SUYÁ.SUY (Brazil)
- - - - Timbira (5): CANELA.RAM (Brazil)
- - - - - GAVIÃO, PARÁ.GAY (Brazil)
- - - - - KRAHÔ.XRA (Brazil)
- - - - - KREYE.XRE (Brazil)
- - - - - KRIKATI-TIMBIRA.XRI (Brazil)
- - Kaingang (3)
- - - Northern (3): KAINGÁNG.KGP (Brazil)
- - - - KAINGANG, SÃO PAULO.ZKS (Brazil)
- - - - XOKLENG.XOK (Brazil)
- Guato (1): GUATÓ.GTA (Brazil)
- Kamakan (1): KAMAKAN.VKM (Brazil)
- Karaja (1): KARAJÁ.KPJ (Brazil)
- Maxakali (1): MAXAKALÍ.MBL (Brazil)
- Opaye (1): OPAYÉ.OPY (Brazil)
- Oti (1): OTI.OTI (Brazil)
- Puri (1): PURI.PRR (Brazil)
- Rikbaktsa (1): RIKBAKTSA.ART (Brazil)
- Yabuti (2): ARIKAPÚ.ARK (Brazil)
- - JABUTÍ.JBT (Brazil)

Maku (5): CACUA.CBV (Colombia)
- HUPDÉ.JUP (Brazil)
- KAMÃ.KWA (Brazil)
- NADËB.MBJ (Brazil)
- YUHUP.YAB (Brazil)

Mascoian (6): ANGAITE.AIV (Paraguay)
- EMOK.EMO (Paraguay)
- GUANA.GVA (Paraguay)
- LENGUA.LEG (Paraguay)
- SANAPANÁ.SAP (Paraguay)
- TOBA-MASKOY.TMF (Paraguay)

Mataco-Guaicuru (11)
- Guaicuruan (4): KADIWÉU.KBC (Brazil)
- - MOCOVÍ.MOC (Argentina)
- - PILAGÁ.PLG (Argentina)
- - TOBA.TOB (Argentina)
- Mataco (7): CHOROTE, IYO'WUJWA.CRQ (Argentina)
- - CHOROTE, IYOJWA'JA.CRT (Argentina)
- - CHULUPÍ.CAG (Paraguay)
- - MACA.MCA (Paraguay)
- - WICHÍ LHAMTÉS GÜISNAY.MZH (Argentina)
- - WICHÍ LHAMTÉS NOCTEN.MTP (Bolivia)
- - WICHÍ LHAMTÉS VEJOZ.MAD (Argentina)

Mayan (68)
- Cholan-Tzeltalan (12)
- - Cholan (4)
- - - Chol-Chontal (3): CHOL, TILA.CTI (Mexico)
- - - - CHOL, TUMBALÁ.CTU (Mexico)
- - - CHONTAL OF TABASCO.CHF (Mexico)
- - - Chorti (1): CHORTÍ.CAA (Guatemala)
- - Tzeltalan (8): TZELTAL, BACHAJÓN.TZB (Mexico)
- - - TZELTAL, HIGHLAND.TZH (Mexico)
- - - TZOTZIL, CH'ENALHÓ.TZE (Mexico)
- - - TZOTZIL, CHAMULA.TZC (Mexico)
- - - TZOTZIL, HUIXTÁN.TZU (Mexico)
- - - TZOTZIL, SAN ANDRÉS LARRAINZAR.TZS (Mexico)
- - - TZOTZIL, VENUSTIANO CARRANZA.TZO (Mexico)
- - - TZOTZIL, ZINACANTECO.TZZ (Mexico)
- Huastecan (4): CHICOMUCELTEC.COB (Mexico)
- - HUASTECO, SAN LUIS POTOSÍ.HVA (Mexico)
- - HUASTECO, SOUTHEASTERN.HAU (Mexico)

Mayan (68)
- Huastecan (4): HUASTECO, VERACRUZ.HUS (Mexico)
- Kanjobalan-Chujean (8)
- - Chujean (3): CHUJ, SAN MATEO IXTATÁN.CNM (Guatemala)
- - - CHUJ, SAN SEBASTIÁN COATÁN.CAC (Guatemala)
- - - TOJOLABAL.TOJ (Mexico)
- - Kanjobalan (5)
- - - Kanjobal-Jacaltec (4): JACALTECO, EASTERN.JAC (Guatemala)
- - - - JACALTECO, WESTERN.JAI (Guatemala)
- - - - KANJOBAL, EASTERN.KJB (Guatemala)
- - - - KANJOBAL, WESTERN.KNJ (Guatemala)
- - - Mocho (1): MOCHO.MHC (Mexico)
- Quichean-Mamean (39)
- - Greater Mamean (11)
- - - Ixilan (4): AGUACATECO.AGU (Guatemala)
- - - - IXIL, CHAJUL.IXJ (Guatemala)
- - - - IXIL, NEBAJ.IXI (Guatemala)
- - - - IXIL, SAN JUAN COTZAL.IXL (Guatemala)
- - - Mamean (7): MAM, CENTRAL.MVC (Guatemala)
- - - - MAM, NORTHERN.MAM (Guatemala)
- - - - MAM, SOUTHERN.MMS (Guatemala)
- - - - MAM, TAJUMULCO.MPF (Guatemala)
- - - - MAM, TODOS SANTOS CUCHUMATÁN.MVJ (Guatemala)
- - - - TACANECO.MTZ (Guatemala)
- - - - TECTITECO.TTC (Guatemala)
- - Greater Quichean (28)
- - - Kekchi (1): KEKCHÍ.KEK (Guatemala)
- - - Pocom (5): POKOMAM, CENTRAL.POC (Guatemala)
- - - - POKOMAM, EASTERN.POA (Guatemala)
- - - - POKOMAM, SOUTHERN.POU (Guatemala)
- - - - POKOMCHÍ, EASTERN.POH (Guatemala)
- - - - POKOMCHÍ, WESTERN.POB (Guatemala)
- - - Quichean (19)
- - - - Cakchiquel (9): CAKCHIQUEL, CENTRAL.CAK (Guatemala)
- - - - - CAKCHIQUEL, EASTERN.CKE (Guatemala)
- - - - - CAKCHIQUEL, NORTHERN.CKC (Guatemala)
- - - - - CAKCHIQUEL, SANTA MARÍA DE JESÚS.CKI (Guatemala)
- - - - - CAKCHIQUEL, SANTO DOMINGO XENACOJ.CKJ (Guatemala)
- - - - - CAKCHIQUEL, SOUTH CENTRAL.CKD (Guatemala)
- - - - - CAKCHIQUEL, SOUTHERN.CKF (Guatemala)
- - - - - CAKCHIQUEL, SOUTHWESTERN, YEPOCAPA.CBM (Guatemala)
- - - - - CAKCHIQUEL, WESTERN.CKW (Guatemala)
- - - - Quiche-Achi (8): ACHÍ, CUBULCO.ACC (Guatemala)
- - - - - ACHÍ, RABINAL.ACR (Guatemala)
- - - - - QUICHÉ, CENTRAL.QUC (Guatemala)
- - - - - QUICHÉ, CUNÉN.CUN (Guatemala)
- - - - - QUICHÉ, EASTERN, CHICHICASTENANGO.QUU (Guatemala)
- - - - - QUICHÉ, JOYABAJ.QUJ (Guatemala)
- - - - - QUICHÉ, SAN ANDRÉS.QIE (Guatemala)
- - - - - QUICHÉ, WEST CENTRAL.QUT (Guatemala)
- - - - Tzutujil (2): TZUTUJIL, EASTERN.TZJ (Guatemala)
- - - - - TZUTUJIL, WESTERN.TZT (Guatemala)
- - - Sacapulteco (1): SACAPULTECO.QUV (Guatemala)
- - - Sipacapeno (1): SIPACAPENSE.QUM (Guatemala)
- - - Uspantec (1): USPANTECO.USP (Guatemala)
- Yucatecan (5)
- - Mopan-Itza (2): ITZÁ.ITZ (Guatemala)
- - - MOPÁN MAYA.MOP (Belize)
- - Yucatec-Lacandon (3): LACANDÓN.LAC (Mexico)
- - - MAYA, CHAN SANTA CRUZ.YUS (Mexico)
- - - MAYA.YUA (Mexico)

Misumalpan (4): CACAOPERA.CCR (El Salvador)
- MATAGALPA.MTN (Nicaragua)
- MÍSKITO.MIQ (Nicaragua)
- SUMO.SUM (Nicaragua)

Mixe-Zoque (16)
- Mixe (9)
- - Eastern Mixe (5): MIXE, COATLÁN.MCO (Mexico)
- - - MIXE, GUICHICOVI.MIR (Mexico)
- - - MIXE, JUQUILA.MXQ (Mexico)
- - - MIXE, MAZATLÁN.MZL (Mexico)
- - - MIXE, NORTHEASTERN.MVE (Mexico)
- - Veracruz Mixe (2): POPOLUCA, OLUTA.PLO (Mexico)
- - - POPOLUCA, SAYULA.POS (Mexico)
- - Western Mixe (2): MIXE, TLAHUITOLTEPEC.MXP (Mexico)
- - - MIXE, TOTONTEPEC.MTO (Mexico)
- Zoque (7)
- - Chiapas Zoque (3): ZOQUE, COPAINALÁ.ZOC (Mexico)
- - - ZOQUE, FRANCISCO LEÓN.ZOS (Mexico)
- - - ZOQUE, RAYÓN.ZOR (Mexico)
- - Oaxaca Zoque (1): ZOQUE, SANTA MARÍA CHIMALAPA.ZOH (Mexico)
- - Veracruz Zoque (3): POPOLUCA, SIERRA.POI (Mexico)
- - - POPOLUCA, TEXISTEPEC.POQ (Mexico)
- - - ZOQUE, TABASCO.ZOQ (Mexico)

Mosetenan (1): TSIMANÉ.CAS (Bolivia)

Mura (1): MÚRA-PIRAHÃ.MYP (Brazil)

Muskogean (6)
- Eastern (4): ALABAMA.AKZ (USA)
- - KOASATI.CKU (USA)
- - MIKASUKI.MIK (USA)
- - MUSKOGEE.CRK (USA)
- Western (2): CHICKASAW.CIC (USA)
- - CHOCTAW.CCT (USA)

Na-Dene (42)
- Haida (1): HAIDA.HAI (Canada)
- Nuclear Na-Dene (41)
- - Athapaskan-Eyak (40)
- - - Athapaskan (39)
- - - - Apachean (6)
- - - - - Kiowa Apache (1): APACHE, KIOWA.APK (USA)
- - - - - Navajo-Apache (5)
- - - - - - Eastern Apache (3): APACHE, JICARILLA.APJ (USA)
- - - - - - - APACHE, LIPAN.APL (USA)
- - - - - - - APACHE, MESCALERO-CHIRICAHUA.APM (USA)
- - - - - - Western Apache-Navajo (2): APACHE, WESTERN.APW (USA)
- - - - - - - NAVAHO.NAV (USA)
- - - - Canadian (12)
- - - - - Beaver-Sekani (2): BEAVER.BEA (Canada)
- - - - - - SEKANI.SEK (Canada)
- - - - - Carrier-Chilcotin (4)
- - - - - - Babine-Carrier (3): BABINE.BCR (Canada)
- - - - - - - CARRIER, SOUTHERN.CAF (Canada)
- - - - - - - CARRIER.CAR (Canada)
- - - - - - Chilcotin (1): CHILCOTIN.CHI (Canada)
- - - - - Han-Kutchin (2): GWICH'IN.KUC (USA)
- - - - - - HAN.HAA (USA)
- - - - - Hare-Chipewyan (3)
- - - - - - Chipewyan (1): CHIPEWYAN.CPW (Canada)
- - - - - - Hare-Slave (2): DOGRIB.DGB (Canada)
- - - - - - - SLAVEY.SLA (Canada)
- - - - - Sarcee (1): SARSI.SRS (Canada)
- - - - Ingalik-Koyukon (3)
- - - - - Ingalik (1): DEGEXIT'AN.ING (USA)
- - - - - Koyukon-Holikachuk (2): HOLIKACHUK.HOI (USA)
- - - - - - KOYUKON.KOY (USA)
- - - - Pacific Coast (9)
- - - - - California (4)
- - - - - - Hupa (1): HUPA.HUP (USA)
- - - - - - Mattole-Wailaki (3): KATO.KTW (USA)
- - - - - - - MATTOLE.MVB (USA)

Niger-Congo (1436)
- Atlantic-Congo (1347)
- - Atlantic (65)
- - - Northern (47)
- - - - Eastern Senegal-Guinea (9)
- - - - - Tenda (5): BASARI.BSC (Guinea)
- - - - - - BIAFADA.BIF (Guinea Bissau)
- - - - - - BUDIK.TNR (Senegal)
- - - - - - WAMEI.COU (Senegal)
- - - - - Mbulungish-Nalu (3): BAGA MBOTENI.BGM (Guinea)
- - - - - MBULUNGISH.MBV (Guinea)
- - - - - NALU.NAJ (Guinea)
- - - - Senegambian (14)
- - - - - Fula-Wolof (13)
- - - - - - Fulani (11)
- - - - - - - East Central (2): FULFULDE, KANO-KATSINA-BORORRO.FUV (Nigeria)
- - - - - - - - FULFULDE, SOKOTO.FUQ (Nigeria)
- - - - - - - Eastern (2): FULFULDE, ADAMAWA.FUB (Cameroon)
- - - - - - - - FULFULDE, BAGIRMI.FUI (Chad)
- - - - - - - West Central (6): FULFULDE, BARANI.FUP (Burkina Faso)
- - - - - - - - FULFULDE, BENIN-TOGO.FUE (Benin)
- - - - - - - - FULFULDE, GOURMANTCHE.FUH (Burkina Faso)
- - - - - - - - FULFULDE, JELGOORE.FUM (Burkina Faso)
- - - - - - - - FULFULDE, MAASINA.FUL (Mali)
- - - - - - - - FUUTA JALON.FUF (Guinea)
- - - - - - - Western (1): FULFULDE, PULAAR.FUC (Senegal)
- - - - - - Wolof (2): WOLOF, GAMBIAN.WOF (Gambia)
- - - - - - WOLOF.WOL (Senegal)
- - - - - Serer (1): SERERE-SINE.SES (Senegal)
- - - Southern (17)
- - - - Limba (2): LIMBA, EAST.LMA (Guinea)
- - - - LIMBA, WEST-CENTRAL.LIA (Sierra Leone)
- - - - Mel (14)
- - - - - Bullom-Kissi (6)
- - - - - - Bullom (4)
- - - - - - - Northern (2): BOM.BMF (Sierra Leone)
- - - - - - - - BULLOM SO.BUY (Sierra Leone)
- - - - - - - Southern (2): KRIM.KRM (Sierra Leone)
- - - - - - - - SHERBRO.BUN (Sierra Leone)
- - - - - Kissi (2): KISI, SOUTHERN.KSS (Liberia)
- - - - - - KISSI, NORTHERN.KQS (Guinea)
- - - - - Gola (1): GOLA.GOL (Liberia)
- - - - - Temne (7)
- - - - - - Baga (6): BAGA BINARI.BCG (Guinea)
- - - - - - - BAGA KOGA.BGO (Guinea)
- - - - - - - BAGA MADURI.BMD (Guinea)
- - - - - - - BAGA SITEMU.BSP (Guinea)
- - - - - - - BAGA SOBANÉ.BSV (Guinea)
- - - - - - - LANDOMA.LAO (Guinea)
- - - - - - Temne-Banta (1): THEMNE.TEJ (Sierra Leone)
- - - Sua (1): MANSOANKA.MSW (Guinea Bissau)
- - Ijoid (10)
- - - Defaka (1): DEFAKA.AFN (Nigeria)
- - - Ijo (9)
- - - - Central (4)
- - - - - Central Western (1): IJO, CENTRAL-WESTERN.IJC (Nigeria)
- - - - - Oruma-Northeast Central (3)
- - - - - - Northeast Central (2): BISENI.IJE (Nigeria)
- - - - - - - OKODIA.OKD (Nigeria)
- - - - - - Oruma (1): ORUMA.ORR (Nigeria)
- - - - - Eastern (5)
- - - - - Northeastern (4)
- - - - - - Ibani-Okrika-Kalabari (3): IBANI.IBY (Nigeria)
- - - - - - - KALABARI.IJN (Nigeria)
- - - - - - - OKRIKA.OKR (Nigeria)
- - - - - Nkoroo (1): NKOROO.NKX (Nigeria)
- - - - Southeastern (1): IJO, SOUTHEAST.IJO (Nigeria)
- - Volta-Congo (1272)
- - - Benue-Congo (895)

Niger-Congo (1436)
- Atlantic-Congo (1347)
- - Volta-Congo (1272)
- - - Benue-Congo (895)
- - - - Bantoid (646)
- - - - - Southern (625)
- - - - - - Narrow Bantu (489)
- - - - - - - Central (319)
- - - - - - - - G (33)
- - - - - - - - - Zigula-Zaramo (G.30) (12): DOE.DOE (Tanzania)
- - - - - - - - - - KAMI.KCU (Tanzania)
- - - - - - - - - - KUTU.KDC (Tanzania)
- - - - - - - - - - KWERE.CWE (Tanzania)
- - - - - - - - - - MUSHUNGULU.XMA (Somalia)
- - - - - - - - - - NGHWELE.NHE (Tanzania)
- - - - - - - - - - NGULU.NGP (Tanzania)
- - - - - - - - - - RUGURU.RUF (Tanzania)
- - - - - - - - - - SAGALA.SBM (Tanzania)
- - - - - - - - - - VIDUNDA.VID (Tanzania)
- - - - - - - - - - ZALAMO.ZAJ (Tanzania)
- - - - - - - - - - ZIGULA.ZIW (Tanzania)
- - - - - - - - - H (19)
- - - - - - - - - - Hungana (H.40) (1): HUNGANA.HUM (Zaïre)
- - - - - - - - - - Kongo (H.10) (7): BEEMBE.BEJ (Congo)
- - - - - - - - - - DOONDO.DOD (Congo)
- - - - - - - - - - KONGO, SAN SALVADOR.KWY (Zaïre)
- - - - - - - - - - KONGO.KON (Zaïre)
- - - - - - - - - - KUNYI.KNF (Congo)
- - - - - - - - - - VILI.VIF (Congo)
- - - - - - - - - - YOMBE.YOM (Zaïre)
- - - - - - - - - - Mbundu (H.20) (4): BOLO.BLV (Angola)
- - - - - - - - - - MBUNDU, LOANDA.MLO (Angola)
- - - - - - - - - - NSONGO.NSX (Angola)
- - - - - - - - - - SAMA.SMD (Angola)
- - - - - - - - - - Yaka (H.30) (7): LONZO.LNZ (Zaïre)
- - - - - - - - - - MBANGALA.MXG (Angola)
- - - - - - - - - - NGONGO.NOQ (Zaïre)
- - - - - - - - - - PELENDE.PPP (Zaïre)
- - - - - - - - - - SONDE.SHC (Zaïre)
- - - - - - - - - - SUKU.SUB (Zaïre)
- - - - - - - - - - YAKA.YAF (Zaïre)
- - - - - - - - - J (48)
- - - - - - - - - - Haya-Jita (J.20) (9): HAYA.HAY (Tanzania)
- - - - - - - - - - HIMA.HIM (Rwanda)
- - - - - - - - - - JITA.JIT (Tanzania)
- - - - - - - - - - KARA.REG (Tanzania)
- - - - - - - - - - KEREBE.KED (Tanzania)
- - - - - - - - - - KWAYA.KYA (Tanzania)
- - - - - - - - - - NYAMBO.NYM (Tanzania)
- - - - - - - - - - TALINGA-BWISI.TLJ (Uganda)
- - - - - - - - - - ZINZA.JIN (Tanzania)
- - - - - - - - - - Konzo (J.40) (5): GBATI-RI.GTI (Zaïre)
- - - - - - - - - - KONJO.KOO (Uganda)
- - - - - - - - - - MAYEKA.MYC (Zaïre)
- - - - - - - - - - NANDI.NNB (Zaïre)
- - - - - - - - - - NYANGA-LI.NYC (Zaïre)
- - - - - - - - - - Masaba-Luyia (J.30) (8)
- - - - - - - - - - Luyia (6): BUKUSU.BUL (Kenya)
- - - - - - - - - - - IDAKHO-ISUKHA-TIRIKI.IDA (Kenya)
- - - - - - - - - - - LOGOOLI.RAG (Kenya)
- - - - - - - - - - - LUYIA.LUY (Kenya)
- - - - - - - - - - - NYORE.NYD (Kenya)
- - - - - - - - - - - SAAMIA.SBU (Kenya)
- - - - - - - - - - MASABA.MYX (Uganda)
- - - - - - - - - - NYOLE.NUJ (Uganda)
- - - - - - - - - - Nyoro-Ganda (J.10) (12): CHIGA.CHG (Uganda)
- - - - - - - - - - GANDA.LAP (Uganda)
- - - - - - - - - - GUNGU.RUB (Uganda)
- - - - - - - - - - GWERE.GWR (Uganda)

Niger-Congo (1436)
- Atlantic-Congo (1347)
- - Volta-Congo (1272)
- - - Benue-Congo (895)
- - - - Bantoid (646)
- - - - - Southern (625)
- - - - - - Narrow Bantu (489)
- - - - - - - Northwest (168)
- - - - - - - - C (71)
- - - - - - - - - Bushong (C.90) (5): BUSHOONG.BUF (Zaïre)
- - - - - - - - - DENGESE.DEZ (Zaïre)
- - - - - - - - - LELE.LEL (Zaïre)
- - - - - - - - - SONGOMENO.SOE (Zaïre)
- - - - - - - - - WONGO.WON (Zaïre)
- - - - - - - - - Kele (C.60) (6): FOMA.FOM (Zaïre)
- - - - - - - - - KELE.KHY (Zaïre)
- - - - - - - - - LOMBO.LOO (Zaïre)
- - - - - - - - - MBESA.ZMS (Zaïre)
- - - - - - - - - POKE.POF (Zaïre)
- - - - - - - - - SO.SOC (Zaïre)
- - - - - - - - - Mbosi (C.30) (6): AKWA.AKW (Congo)
- - - - - - - - - KOYO.KOH (Congo)
- - - - - - - - - LIKUBA.KXX (Congo)
- - - - - - - - - LIKWALA.KWC (Congo)
- - - - - - - - - MBOKO.MDU (Congo)
- - - - - - - - - MBOSI.MDW (Congo)
- - - - - - - - - Mongo (C.70) (4): LALIA.LAL (Zaïre)
- - - - - - - - - MONGO-NKUNDU.MOM (Zaïre)
- - - - - - - - - NGANDO.NXD (Zaïre)
- - - - - - - - - OMBO.OML (Zaïre)
- - - - - - - - - Ngando (C.10) (2): NGANDO.NGD (Central African Republic)
- - - - - - - - - YAKA.AXK (Central African Republic)
- - - - - - - - - Ngombe (C.50) (8): BWA.BWW (Zaïre)
- - - - - - - - - BWELA.BWL (Zaïre)
- - - - - - - - - KANGO.KTY (Zaïre)
- - - - - - - - - LIGENZA.LGZ (Zaïre)
- - - - - - - - - NGELIMA.AGH (Zaïre)
- - - - - - - - - NGOMBE.NGC (Zaïre)
- - - - - - - - - PAGABETE.PAG (Zaïre)
- - - - - - - - - TEMBO.TMV (Zaïre)
- - - - - - - - - Ngundi (C.20) (6): BABOLE.BVX (Congo)
- - - - - - - - - BOMITABA.ZMX (Congo)
- - - - - - - - - BONGILI.BUI (Congo)
- - - - - - - - - MBATI.MDN (Central African Republic)
- - - - - - - - - NGUNDI.NDN (Congo)
- - - - - - - - - PANDE.BKJ (Central African Republic)
- - - - - - - - - Tetela (C.80) (5): KELA.KEL (Zaïre)
- - - - - - - - - KUSU.KSV (Zaïre)
- - - - - - - - - NKUTU.NKW (Zaïre)
- - - - - - - - - TETELA.TEL (Zaïre)
- - - - - - - - - YELA.YEL (Zaïre)
- - - - - - - - Unclassified (2): BEMBA.BMY (Zaïre)
- - - - - - - - SONGA.SGO (Zaïre)
- - - - - - - Ndemli (1): NDEMLI.NML (Cameroon)
- - - - - - - Tikar (1): TIKAR.TIK (Cameroon)
- - - - - - - Tivoid (16): ABONG.ABO (Nigeria)
- - - - - - - BALO.BQO (Cameroon)
- - - - - - - BATU.BTU (Nigeria)
- - - - - - - BITARE.BRE (Nigeria)
- - - - - - - CAKA.CKX (Cameroon)
- - - - - - - EMAN.EMN (Cameroon)
- - - - - - - ESIMBI.AGS (Cameroon)
- - - - - - - EVAND.BZZ (Nigeria)
- - - - - - - ICEVE-MACI.BEC (Cameroon)
- - - - - - - IPULO.ASS (Cameroon)
- - - - - - - IYIVE.UIV (Cameroon)
- - - - - - - MANTA.MYG (Cameroon)
- - - - - - - MESAKA.IYO (Cameroon)
- - - - - - - OSATU.OST (Cameroon)

Niger-Congo (1436)
- Atlantic-Congo (1347)
- - Volta-Congo (1272)
- - - Benue-Congo (895)
- - - - Bantoid (646)
- - - - - Southern (625)
- - - - - - Wide Grassfields (62)
- - - - - - - Narrow Grassfields (58)
- - - - - - - - Ring (16)
- - - - - - - - - North (4): KENSWEI NSEI.NDB (Cameroon)
- - - - - - - - - VENGO.BAV (Cameroon)
- - - - - - - - - WUSHI.BSE (Cameroon)
- - - - - - - - - West (6): AGHEM.AGQ (Cameroon)
- - - - - - - - - FUNGOM.FUG (Cameroon)
- - - - - - - - - ISU.ISU (Cameroon)
- - - - - - - - - LAIMBUE.LMX (Cameroon)
- - - - - - - - - OSO.OSO (Cameroon)
- - - - - - - - - WEH.WEH (Cameroon)
- - - - - - - Western Momo (3): AMBELE.AEL (Cameroon)
- - - - - - - - ATONG.ATO (Cameroon)
- - - - - - - - BUSAM.BXS (Cameroon)
- - - - - Unclassified (3): BURU.BQW (Nigeria)
- - - - - - BUSUU.BJU (Cameroon)
- - - - - - CUNG.CUG (Cameroon)
- - - - Cross River (63)
- - - - - Bendi (9): ALEGE.ALF (Nigeria)
- - - - - - BEKWARRA.BKV (Nigeria)
- - - - - - BETE-BENDE.BTT (Nigeria)
- - - - - - BOKYI.BKY (Nigeria)
- - - - - - BUMAJI.BYP (Nigeria)
- - - - - - OBANLIKU.BZY (Nigeria)
- - - - - - UBANG.UBA (Nigeria)
- - - - - - UKPE-BAYOBIRI.UKP (Nigeria)
- - - - - - UTUGWANG.AFE (Nigeria)
- - - - - Delta Cross (53)
- - - - - - Central Delta (8)
- - - - - - - Abua-Odual (2): ABUA.ABN (Nigeria)
- - - - - - - - ODUAL.ODU (Nigeria)
- - - - - - - Kugbo (6): KUGBO.KES (Nigeria)
- - - - - - - - MINI.MGJ (Nigeria)
- - - - - - - - OBULOM.OBU (Nigeria)
- - - - - - - - OGBIA.OGB (Nigeria)
- - - - - - - - OGBOGOLO.OGG (Nigeria)
- - - - - - - - OGBRONUAGUM.OGU (Nigeria)
- - - - - - Lower Cross (20)
- - - - - - - East (8): ANAANG.ANW (Nigeria)
- - - - - - - - EFAI.EFA (Nigeria)
- - - - - - - - EFIK.EFK (Nigeria)
- - - - - - - - EKIT.EKE (Nigeria)
- - - - - - - - ETEBI.ETB (Nigeria)
- - - - - - - - IBIBIO.IBB (Nigeria)
- - - - - - - - IBUORO.IBR (Nigeria)
- - - - - - - - ITU MBON UZO.ITM (Nigeria)
- - - - - - - Unclassified (7): EBUGHU.EBG (Nigeria)
- - - - - - - - IDERE.IDE (Nigeria)
- - - - - - - - ILUE.ILE (Nigeria)
- - - - - - - - ITO.ITW (Nigeria)
- - - - - - - - UDA.UDA (Nigeria)
- - - - - - - - UKWA.UKQ (Nigeria)
- - - - - - - - USAKADE.USK (Nigeria)
- - - - - - - West (5): IBINO.IBN (Nigeria)
- - - - - - - - IKO.IKI (Nigeria)
- - - - - - - - OBOLO.ANN (Nigeria)
- - - - - - - - OKOBO.OKB (Nigeria)
- - - - - - - - ORON.ORX (Nigeria)
- - - - - - Ogoni (3)
- - - - - - - East (2): GOKANA.GKN (Nigeria)
- - - - - - - - KOANA.KEH (Nigeria)
- - - - - - - West (1): ELEME.ELM (Nigeria)

- Osse (3): IYAYU.IYA (Nigeria)
- - - - - - UHAMI.UHA (Nigeria)
- - - - - - UKUE-EHUEN.UKU (Nigeria)
- - - - - - Southern (2): OKPAMHERI.OPA (Nigeria)
- - - - - - OKPE-IDESA-OLOMA-AKUKU.OKP (Nigeria)
- - - - - ADUGE.ADU (Nigeria)
- - - - - Southwestern (5): ERUWA.ERH (Nigeria)
- - - - - ISOKO.ISO (Nigeria)
- - - - - OKPE.OKE (Nigeria)
- - - - - URHOBO.URH (Nigeria)
- - - - - UVBIE.EVH (Nigeria)
- - - - Idomoid (9)
- - - - - Akweya (7)
- - - - - Eloyi (1): ELOYI.AFO (Nigeria)
- - - - - Etulo-Idoma (6)
- - - - - - Etulo (1): ETULO.UTR (Nigeria)
- - - - - - Idoma (5): AGATU.AGC (Nigeria)
- - - - - - - ALAGO.ALA (Nigeria)
- - - - - - - IDOMA.IDO (Nigeria)
- - - - - - - IGEDE.IGE (Nigeria)
- - - - - - - YALA.YBA (Nigeria)
- - - - - Yatye-Akpa (2): AKPA.AKF (Nigeria)
- - - - - - EKPARI.EKR (Nigeria)
- - - - Igboid (7)
- - - - - Ekpeye (1): EKPEYE.EKP (Nigeria)
- - - - - Igbo (6): IGBO.IGR (Nigeria)
- - - - - IKA.IKK (Nigeria)
- - - - - IKWERE.IKW (Nigeria)
- - - - - IZI-EZAA-IKWO-MGBO.IZI (Nigeria)
- - - - - OGBAH.OGC (Nigeria)
- - - - - UKWUANI-ABOH.UKW (Nigeria)
- - - - Kainji (55)
- - - - Eastern (31)
- - - - - Amo (1): AMO.AMO (Nigeria)
- - - - - Northern Jos (28)
- - - - - - Jera (15): DUGUZA.DZA (Nigeria)
- - - - - - GAMO-NINGI.BTE (Nigeria)
- - - - - - GANA.GNH (Nigeria)
- - - - - - GYEM.GYE (Nigeria)
- - - - - - IGUTA.NAR (Nigeria)
- - - - - - IZORA.CBO (Nigeria)
- - - - - - JANJI.JNI (Nigeria)
- - - - - - JERA.JER (Nigeria)
- - - - - - KUDU-CAMO.KOV (Nigeria)
- - - - - - LEMORO.LDJ (Nigeria)
- - - - - - SANGA.SGA (Nigeria)
- - - - - - SHAU.SQH (Nigeria)
- - - - - - SHENI.SCV (Nigeria)
- - - - - - TAURA.TDM (Nigeria)
- - - - - - ZIRIYA.ZIR (Nigeria)
- - - - - - Kauru (13): BINA.BYJ (Nigeria)
- - - - - - DUNGU.DBV (Nigeria)
- - - - - - GBIRI-NIRAGU.GRH (Nigeria)
- - - - - - KAIVI.KCE (Nigeria)
- - - - - - KIBALLO.KCH (Nigeria)
- - - - - - KINUKU.KKD (Nigeria)
- - - - - - KITIMI.KKU (Nigeria)
- - - - - - KONO.KLK (Nigeria)
- - - - - - KURAMA.KRH (Nigeria)
- - - - - - KUZAMANI.KSA (Nigeria)
- - - - - - MALA.RUY (Nigeria)
- - - - - - RUMA.RUZ (Nigeria)
- - - - - - SURUBU.SDE (Nigeria)
- - - - - Piti-Atsam (2): ATSAM.CCH (Nigeria)
- - - - - - PITI.PCN (Nigeria)
- - - - Western (24)
- - - - - Basa (3): BASA-KADUNA.BSL (Nigeria)
- - - - - - BASSA-KONTAGORA.BSR (Nigeria)
- - - - - - RUBASA.BZW (Nigeria)

Niger-Congo (1436)
- Atlantic-Congo (1347)
- - Volta-Congo (1272)
- - - Kru (41)
- - - - Eastern (11)
- - - - - Dida (3): NEYO.NEY (Côte d'Ivoire)
- - - - - Kwadia (1): KODIA.KWP (Côte d'Ivoire)
- - - - Kuwaa (1): KUWAA.BLH (Liberia)
- - - - Seme (1): SIAMOU.SIF (Burkina Faso)
- - - - Western (26)
- - - - - Bassa (3): BASSA.BAS (Liberia)
- - - - - - DEWOIN.DEE (Liberia)
- - - - - - GBII.GGB (Liberia)
- - - - - Grebo (13)
- - - - - - Glio-Oubi (1): GLIO-OUBI.OUB (Liberia)
- - - - - - Ivoirian (1): KRUMEN, PLAPO.KTJ (Côte d'Ivoire)
- - - - - - Ivorian (2): KRUMEN, PYE.PYE (Côte d'Ivoire)
- - - - - - - KRUMEN, TEPO.TED (Côte d'Ivoire)
- - - - - - Liberian (9): GREBO, BARCLAYVILLE.GRY (Liberia)
- - - - - - - GREBO, E JE.GRB (Liberia)
- - - - - - - GREBO, FOPO-BUA.GEF (Liberia)
- - - - - - - GREBO, GBOLOO.GEC (Liberia)
- - - - - - - GREBO, GLEBO.GEU (Liberia)
- - - - - - - GREBO, GLOBO.GRV (Liberia)
- - - - - - - GREBO, JABO.GRJ (Liberia)
- - - - - - - GREBO, NORTHEASTERN.GRP (Liberia)
- - - - - - - GREBO, SEASIDE.GRF (Côte d'Ivoire)
- - - - - Klao (2): KLAO.KLU (Liberia)
- - - - - TAJUASOHN.KRU (Liberia)
- - - - - Wee (8)
- - - - - - Guere-Krahn (5): DAHO-DOO.DAS (Côte d'Ivoire)
- - - - - - - GLARO-TWABO.GLR (Liberia)
- - - - - - - GUÉRÉ, CENTRAL.GXX (Côte d'Ivoire)
- - - - - - - KRAHN, WESTERN.KRW (Liberia)
- - - - - - SAPO.KRN (Liberia)
- - - - - Konobo (1): KRAHN, EASTERN.KQO (Liberia)
- - - - - Nyabwa (1): NYABWA.NIA (Côte d'Ivoire)
- - - - - Wobe (1): WOBE.WOB (Côte d'Ivoire)
- - - Kwa (78)
- - - - Left Bank (29)
- - - - - Avatime-Nyangbo (3): AVATIME.AVA (Ghana)
- - - - - - NYANGBO.NYB (Ghana)
- - - - - - TAFI.TCD (Ghana)
- - - - - Gbe (21)
- - - - - - Aja (9): AJA-GBE.AJG (Benin)
- - - - - - - AYIZO-GBE.AYB (Benin)
- - - - - - - GUN-GBE.GUW (Benin)
- - - - - - - HWÉ.HWE (Togo)
- - - - - - - SETO-GBE.STS (Benin)
- - - - - - - TOFIN-GBE.TFI (Benin)
- - - - - - - TOLI-GBE.TLH (Benin)
- - - - - - - WEME-GBE.WEM (Benin)
- - - - - - - XWLA-GBE.XWL (Benin)
- - - - - - Fon (2): FON-GBE.FOA (Benin)
- - - - - - - MAXI-GBE.MXL (Benin)
- - - - - - Mina (1): GEN-GBE.GEJ (Togo)
- - - - - - CI-GBE.CIB (Benin)
- - - - - - ÉWÉ.EWE (Ghana)
- - - - - - KO-GBE.KQK (Benin)
- - - - - - KPESSI.KEF (Togo)
- - - - - - SAXWE-GBE.SXW (Benin)
- - - - - - WACI-GBE.WCI (Togo)
- - - - - - WUDU.WUD (Togo)
- - - - - - XWEDA-GBE.XWD (Benin)
- - - - - - XWELA-GBE.XWE (Benin)
- - - - - Kebu-Animere (2): AKEBOU.KEU (Togo)
- - - - - - ANIMERE.ANF (Ghana)
- - - - - Kposo-Ahlo-Bowili (3): AKPOSO.KPO (Togo)
- - - - - - BOWIRI.BOV (Ghana)

Niger-Congo (1436)
- Atlantic-Congo (1347)
- - Volta-Congo (1272)
- - - Kwa (78)
- - - - Left Bank (29)
- - - - - Kposo-Ahlo-Bowili (3): IGO.AHL (Togo)
- - - - Nyo (47)
- - - - - Agneby (3): ABÉ.ABA (Côte d'Ivoire)
- - - - - - ABIDJI.ABI (Côte d'Ivoire)
- - - - - - ADIOUKROU.ADJ (Côte d'Ivoire)
- - - - - Attie (1): ATTIÉ.ATI (Côte d'Ivoire)
- - - - - Avikam-Alladian (2): ALADIAN.ALD (Côte d'Ivoire)
- - - - - - AVIKAM.AVI (Côte d'Ivoire)
- - - - - Ga-Dangme (1): GA-ADANGME-KROBO.GAC (Ghana)
- - - - - Potou-Tano (39)
- - - - - - Basila-Adele (2): ADELE.ADE (Togo)
- - - - - - - ANII.BLO (Benin)
- - - - - - Ega (1): EGA.DIE (Côte d'Ivoire)
- - - - - - Lelemi (4)
- - - - - - - Lelemi-Akpafu (2): AKPAFU-LOLOBI.AKP (Ghana)
- - - - - - - - LELEMI.LEF (Ghana)
- - - - - - - Likpe-Santrokofi (2): SEKPELE.LIP (Ghana)
- - - - - - - - SELE.SNW (Ghana)
- - - - - - Logba (1): LOGBA.LGQ (Ghana)
- - - - - - Potou (2): EBRIÉ.EBR (Côte d'Ivoire)
- - - - - - - MBATO.GWA (Côte d'Ivoire)
- - - - - - Tano (28)
- - - - - - - Central (12)
- - - - - - - - Akan (4): ABRON.ABR (Ghana)
- - - - - - - - - AKAN.TWS (Ghana)
- - - - - - - - - BASA.BQA (Benin)
- - - - - - - - - WASA.WSS (Ghana)
- - - - - - - - Bia (8)
- - - - - - - - - Northern (5): ANUFO.CKO (Ghana)
- - - - - - - - - - ANYIN, MOROFO.MTB (Côte d'Ivoire)
- - - - - - - - - - ANYIN.ANY (Côte d'Ivoire)
- - - - - - - - - - BAULE.BCI (Côte d'Ivoire)
- - - - - - - - - - SEHWI.SFW (Ghana)
- - - - - - - - - Southern (3): AHANTA.AHA (Ghana)
- - - - - - - - - - JWIRA-PEPESA.JWI (Ghana)
- - - - - - - - - - NZEMA.NZE (Ghana)
- - - - - - - Guang (13)
- - - - - - - - North Guang (11): ANYANGA.AYG (Togo)
- - - - - - - - - CHUMBURUNG.NCU (Ghana)
- - - - - - - - - DWANG.NNU (Ghana)
- - - - - - - - - FOODO.FOD (Benin)
- - - - - - - - - GIKYODE.ACD (Ghana)
- - - - - - - - - GONJA.DUM (Ghana)
- - - - - - - - - KPLANG.PRA (Ghana)
- - - - - - - - - KRACHE.KYE (Ghana)
- - - - - - - - - NAWURI.NAW (Ghana)
- - - - - - - - - NCHUMBULU.NLU (Ghana)
- - - - - - - - - NKONYA.NKO (Ghana)
- - - - - - - - South Guang (2): AWUTU.AFU (Ghana)
- - - - - - - - - GUA.LAR (Ghana)
- - - - - - - Krobu (1): KROBU.KXB (Côte d'Ivoire)
- - - - - - - Western (2): ABURE.ABU (Côte d'Ivoire)
- - - - - - - - BETI.EOT (Côte d'Ivoire)
- - - - - - Unclassified (1): AKPE.AQP (Togo)
- - - - - Unclassified (1): ESUMA.ESM (Côte d'Ivoire)
- - - - Unclassified (2): AIZI, APROUMU.AHP (Côte d'Ivoire)
- - - - CENKA.CEN (Benin)
- - North (257)
- - - Adamawa-Ubangi (157)
- - - - Adamawa (86)
- - - - - Fali (2): FALI, NORTH.FLL (Cameroon)
- - - - - - FALI, SOUTH.FAL (Cameroon)
- - - - - Gueve (1): GEY.GUV (Cameroon)
- - - - - Kam (1): KAM.KDX (Nigeria)

Niger-Congo (1436)
- Atlantic-Congo (1347)
- - Volta-Congo (1272)
- - - North (257)
- - - - Adamawa-Ubangi (157)
- - - - - Adamawa (86)
- - - - - - Mbum-Day (30)
- - - - - - - Mbum (16)
- - - - - - - - Northern (6)
- - - - - - - - - Tupuri-Mambai (3): TUPURI.TUI (Cameroon)
- - - - - - - - - Southern (1): MBUM.MDD (Cameroon)
" - - - - - - - - Unclassified (4): DEK.DEK (Cameroon)
- - - - - - - - - LAKA.LAK (Nigeria)
" - - - - - - - - PAM.PMN (Cameroon)
" - - - - - - - - TO.TOZ (Cameroon)
- - - - - - - Unclassified (1): OBLO.OBL (Cameroon)
- - - - - - Waja-Jen (22)
- - - - - - - Jen (9): BURAK.BYS (Nigeria)
- - - - - - - - DZA.JEN (Nigeria)
- - - - - - - - GWOMU.GWG (Nigeria)
- - - - - - - - KYAK.BKA (Nigeria)
- - - - - - - - LEELAU.LDK (Nigeria)
- - - - - - - - LO.LDO (Nigeria)
- - - - - - - - MÁGHDÌ.GMD (Nigeria)
- - - - - - - - MAK.PBL (Nigeria)
- - - - - - - - MUNGA.MKO (Nigeria)
- - - - - - - Longuda (1): LONGUDA.LNU (Nigeria)
- - - - - - - Waja (8)
- - - - - - - - Awak (2): AWAK.AWO (Nigeria)
- - - - - - - - - KAMO.KCQ (Nigeria)
- - - - - - - - Cham-Mona (2): DIJIM.CFA (Nigeria)
- - - - - - - - - LOTSU-PIRI.LDP (Nigeria)
- - - - - - - - Dadiya (1): DADIYA.DBD (Nigeria)
- - - - - - - - Tula (3): BANGWINJI.BSJ (Nigeria)
- - - - - - - - - TULA.TUL (Nigeria)
- - - - - - - - - WAJA.WJA (Nigeria)
" " " " " " " Yungur (4)
- - - - - - - - Libo (1): LIBO.LDL (Nigeria)
- - - - - - - - Mboi (1): MBOI.MOI (Nigeria)
- - - - - - - - Yungur-Roba (2): LALA-ROBA.LLA (Nigeria)
- - - - - - - - - YUNGUR.YUN (Nigeria)
- - - - - Ubangi (71)
- - - - - - Banda (17)
- - - - - - - Central (11)
- - - - - - - - Central Core (10)
- - - - - - - - - Banda-Bambari (1): BANDA-BAMBARI.LIY (Central African Republic)
- - - - - - - - - Banda-Banda (1): BANDA-BANDA.BPD (Central African Republic)
- - - - - - - - - Banda-Mbres (1): BANDA-MBRÈS.BQK (Central African Republic)
- - - - - - - - - Banda-Ndele (1): BANDA-NDÉLÉ.BFL (Central African Republic)
- - - - - - - - - Mid-Southern (5): BANDA, MID-SOUTHERN.BJO (Central African Republic)
- - - - - - - - - - GUBU.GOX (Zaïre)
- - - - - - - - - - KPAGUA.KUW (Zaïre)
- - - - - - - - - - MONO.MNH (Zaïre)
- - - - - - - - - - NGUNDU.NUE (Zaïre)
- - - - - - - - - Togbo-Vara (1): BANDA, TOGBO-VARA.TOR (Zaïre)
- - - - - - - - Western (1): BANDA-YANGERE.YAJ (Central African Republic)
- - - - - - - South Central (2): BANDA, SOUTH CENTRAL.LNL (Central African Republic)
- - - - - - - - LANGBASHE.LNA (Central African Republic)
- - - - - - - Southern (1): MBANZA.ZMZ (Zaïre)
- - - - - - - Southwestern (1): NGBUNDU.NUU (Zaïre)
- - - - - - - West Central (2): BANDA, WEST CENTRAL.BBP (Central African Republic)
- - - - - - - - BANDA, WEST CENTRAL.BBP (Sudan)
- - - - - - Gbaya (1)
- - - - - - - Gbaya (1): MBODOMO.QMF (Cameroon)
- - - - - - Gbaya-Manza-Ngbaka (14)
- - - - - - - Central (4): BOKOTO.BDT (Central African Republic)
- - - - - - - - GBANU.GBV (Central African Republic)
- - - - - - - - GBAYA-BOSSANGOA.GBP (Central African Republic)
- - - - - - - - GBAYA-BOZOUM.GBQ (Central African Republic)

Niger-Congo (1436)
- Atlantic-Congo (1347)
- - Volta-Congo (1272)
- - - North (257)
- - - - Gur (100)
- - - - - Central (72)
- - - - - - Northern (40)
- - - - - - - Bwamu (4): BWAMU, LAA LAA.BWJ (Burkina Faso)
- - - - - - - - BWAMU, TWI.BWY (Burkina Faso)
- - - - - - - - BWAMU.BOX (Burkina Faso)
- - - - - - - Kurumfe (1): KOROMFÉ.KFZ (Burkina Faso)
- - - - - - - Oti-Volta (35)
- - - - - - - - Buli-Koma (2): BULI.BWU (Ghana)
- - - - - - - - - KONNI.KMA (Ghana)
- - - - - - - - Eastern (5): BIALI.BEH (Benin)
- - - - - - - - - DITAMMARI.TBZ (Benin)
- - - - - - - - - MBELIME.MQL (Benin)
- - - - - - - - - TAMBERMA.SOF (Togo)
- - - - - - - - - WAAMA.WWA (Benin)
- - - - - - - - Gurma (9)
- - - - - - - - - Moba (2): BIMOBA.BIM (Ghana)
- - - - - - - - - - MOBA.MFQ (Togo)
- - - - - - - - - Ntcham (2): AKASELEM.AKS (Togo)
- - - - - - - - - - NTCHAM.BUD (Togo)
- - - - - - - - - GOURMANCHÉMA.GUX (Burkina Faso)
- - - - - - - - - KONKOMBA.KOS (Ghana)
- - - - - - - - - NATENI.NTM (Benin)
- - - - - - - - - NGANGAM.GNG (Togo)
- - - - - - - - - SOLA.SOY (Benin)
- - - - - - - - Western (17)
- - - - - - - - - Nootre (1): BOULBA.BLY (Benin)
- - - - - - - - - Northwest (9)
- - - - - - - - - - Dagaari-Birifor (5)
- - - - - - - - - - - Birifor (2): BIRIFOR, MALBA.BFO (Burkina Faso)
- - - - - - - - - - - - BIRIFOR, SOUTHERN.BIV (Ghana)
- - - - - - - - - - - Dagaari (3): DAGAARI DIOULA.DGD (Burkina Faso)
- - - - - - - - - - - - DAGAARI, SOUTHERN.DGA (Ghana)
- - - - - - - - - - - - DAGARA, NORTHERN.DGI (Burkina Faso)
- - - - - - - - - - MÒORÉ.MHM (Burkina Faso)
- - - - - - - - - - SAFALIBA.SAF (Ghana)
- - - - - - - - - - WALI.WLX (Ghana)
- - - - - - - - - - YANA.YAN (Burkina Faso)
- - - - - - - - - Southeast (7)
- - - - - - - - - - Kusaal (2): KUSAAL, EASTERN.KUS (Ghana)
- - - - - - - - - - - KUSAAL, WESTERN.KNU (Burkina Faso)
- - - - - - - - - - DAGBANI.DAG (Ghana)
- - - - - - - - - - GURENNE.GUR (Ghana)
- - - - - - - - - - HANGA.HAG (Ghana)
- - - - - - - - - - KANTOSI.XKT (Ghana)
- - - - - - - - - - MAMPRULI.MAW (Ghana)
- - - - - - - - - Yom-Nawdm (2): NAWDM.NMZ (Togo)
- - - - - - - - - - PILA.PIL (Benin)
- - - - - - - Southern (32)
- - - - - - - - Dogoso-Khe (2): DOGOSO.DGS (Burkina Faso)
- - - - - - - - - KHE.KQG (Burkina Faso)
- - - - - - - - Dyan (1): DYAN.DYA (Burkina Faso)
- - - - - - - - Gan-Dogose (4): DOGHOSIÉ.DOS (Burkina Faso)
- - - - - - - - - KAANSE.GNA (Burkina Faso)
- - - - - - - - - KHISA.KQM (Côte d'Ivoire)
- - - - - - - - - KPATOGO.GBW (Burkina Faso)
- - - - - - - - Grusi (23)
- - - - - - - - - Eastern (7): BAGO.BQG (Togo)
- - - - - - - - - - CHALA.CHA (Ghana)
- - - - - - - - - - DELO.NTR (Ghana)
- - - - - - - - - - KABIYÉ.KBP (Togo)
- - - - - - - - - - LAMA.LAS (Togo)
- - - - - - - - - - LUKPA.DOP (Benin)
- - - - - - - - - - TEM.KDH (Togo)
- - - - - - - - - Northern (6): KALAMSE.KNZ (Burkina Faso)

Niger-Congo (1436)
- Mande (58)
- - Western (39)
- - - Northwestern (30)
- - - - Northern (23)
- - - - - Greater Mandekan (20)
- - - - - - Mandekan (18)
- - - - - - - Manding (17): MANDINKA.MNK (Senegal)
- - - - - - - - MANINKA.MNI (Guinea)
- - - - - - - - MANYA.MZJ (Liberia)
- - - - - - - - MAOU.MXX (Côte d'Ivoire)
- - - - - - - - MARKA.MWR (Burkina Faso)
- - - - - - - - MIKIFORE.MFG (Guinea)
- - - - - - - - MORI.MRG (Gambia)
- - - - - - Vai-Kono (2): KONO.KNO (Sierra Leone)
- - - - - - - VAI.VAI (Liberia)
- - - - - Ligbi-Numu (1): LIGBI.LIG (Ghana)
- - - - - Susu-Yalunka (2): SUSU.SUD (Guinea)
- - - - - YALUNKA.YAL (Guinea)
- - - Southwestern (7)
- - - - Kpelle (2): KPELLE, GUINEA.GKP (Guinea)
- - - - - KPELLE, LIBERIA.KPE (Liberia)
- - - - Loma-Loko (5)
- - - - - Loko-Mende (3)
- - - - - - Loko (1): LOKO.LOK (Sierra Leone)
- - - - - - Mende-Bandi (2): BANDI.GBA (Liberia)
- - - - - - - MENDE.MFY (Sierra Leone)
- - - - - Loma (2): LOMA.LOM (Liberia)
- - - - - - TOMA.TOD (Guinea)
- - - Sambla-Samogho (1): SEEKU.SOS (Burkina Faso)
- - - Soninke-Bozo (5): BOSO, HAINYAXO.BZX (Mali)
- - - - BOSO, SOROGAMA.BZE (Mali)
- - - - BOSO, TIÉYAXO.BOZ (Mali)
- - - - BOSO, TIÈMA CIÈWÈ.BOO (Mali)
- - - - SONINKE.SNN (Mali)
- - - Unclassified (1): BANKA.BXW (Mali)

Nilo-Saharan (194)
- Berta (2): BERTA.WTI (Sudan)
- - GOBATO.GTO (Ethiopia)
- Central Sudanic (64)
- - East (23)
- - - Lendu (3): BENDI.BCT (Zaïre)
- - - - LENDU.LED (Zaïre)
- - - - NGITI.NIY (Zaïre)
- - - Mangbetu (4): ASUA.ASV (Zaïre)
- - - - LOMBI.LMI (Zaïre)
- - - - MANGBELE.MKQ (Zaïre)
- - - - MANGBETU.MDJ (Zaïre)
- - - Mangbutu-Efe (6): EFE.EFE (Zaïre)
- - - - LESE.LES (Zaïre)
- - - - MAMVU.MDI (Zaïre)
- - - - MANGBUTU.MDK (Zaïre)
- - - - MVUBA.MXH (Zaïre)
- - - - NDO.NDP (Zaïre)
- - - Moru-Madi (10)
- - - - Central (6): ARINGA.LUC (Uganda)
- - - - - AVOKAYA.AVU (Zaïre)
- - - - - KALIKO.KBO (Zaïre)
- - - - - LOGO.LOG (Zaïre)
- - - - - LUGBARA.LUG (Uganda)
- - - - - OMI.OMI (Zaïre)
- - - - Northern (1): MORU.MGD (Sudan)
- - - - Southern (3): LULUBA.LUL (Sudan)
- - - - - MA'DI, SOUTHERN.QMD (Uganda)
- - - - - MA'DI.MHI (Uganda)
- - West (41)
- - - Bongo-Bagirmi (39)
- - - - Bongo-Baka (8)

- Majang (1): MAJANG.MPE (Ethiopia)
- - - - South (9)
- - - - - Southeast (4)
- - - - - - Kwegu (1): KWEGU.YID (Ethiopia)
- - - - - - Pastoral (3)
- - - - - - - Me'en (1): ME'EN.MYM (Ethiopia)
- - - - - - - Suri (2): MURSI.MUZ (Ethiopia)
- - - - - - - - SURI.SUQ (Ethiopia)
- - - - - Southwest (5)
- - - - - - Didinga-Murle (4)
- - - - - - - Didinga-Longarim (2): DIDINGA.DID (Sudan)
- - - - - - - - LONGARIM.LOH (Sudan)
- - - - - - - Murle (1): MURLE.MUR (Sudan)
- - - - - - - Tenet (1): TENNET.TEX (Sudan)
- - - - - - Kacipo-Balesi (1): KACIPO-BALESI.KOE (Sudan)
- - Kuliak (3)
- - - Ik (1): IK.IKX (Uganda)
- - - Ngangea-So (2): NYANG'I.NYP (Uganda)
- - - - SOO.TEU (Uganda)
- - Nilotic (53)
- - - Eastern (17)
- - - Bari (3): BARI.BFA (Sudan)
- - - - KAKWA.KEO (Uganda)
- - - - MANDARI.MQU (Sudan)
- - - Lotuxo-Maa (4)
- - - - Lotuxo (1): OTUHO.LOT (Sudan)
- - - - Ongamo-Maa (3): MAASAI.MET (Kenya)
- - - - - NGASA.NSG (Tanzania)
- - - - - SAMBURU.SAQ (Kenya)
- - - Lotuxo-Teso (4)
- - - - Lotuxo-Maa (4)
- - - - - Lotuxo (4): DONGOTONO.DDD (Sudan)
- - - - - - LANGO.LNO (Sudan)
- - - - - - LOKOYA.LKY (Sudan)
- - - - - - - LOPIT.LPX (Sudan)
- - - - Teso-Turkana (6)
- - - - - Teso (1): TESO.TEO (Uganda)
- - - - - Turkana (4): KARAMOJONG.KDJ (Uganda)
- - - - - - NYANGATOM.NNJ (Ethiopia)
- - - - - - TOPOSA.TOQ (Sudan)
- - - - - - TURKANA.TUV (Kenya)
- - - - Unclassified (1): MENING.MYQ (Uganda)
- - - Southern (14)
- - - - Kalenjin (12)
- - - - - Elgon (2): KUPSABINY.KPZ (Uganda)
- - - - - SABAOT.SPY (Kenya)
- - - - - Nandi-Markweta (8)
- - - - - - Markweta (2): ENDO.ENB (Kenya)
- - - - - - - TALAI.TLE (Kenya)
- - - - - - Nandi (6): ARAMANIK.AAM (Tanzania)
- - - - - - - KALENJIN.KLN (Kenya)
- - - - - - - KISANKASA.KQH (Tanzania)
- - - - - - - MEDIAK.MWX (Tanzania)
- - - - - - - MOSIRO.MWY (Tanzania)
- - - - - - - TUGEN, NORTH.TUY (Kenya)
- - - - - Okiek (1): OKIEK.OKI (Kenya)
- - - - - Pokot (1): PÖKOOT.PKO (Kenya)
- - - - Tatoga (2): DATOOGA.TCC (Tanzania)
- - - - - OMOTIK.OMT (Kenya)
- - - Western (22)
- - - Dinka-Nuer (7)
- - - - Dinka (5): DINKA, NORTHEASTERN.DIP (Sudan)
- - - - - DINKA, NORTHWESTERN.DIW (Sudan)
- - - - - DINKA, SOUTH CENTRAL.DIB (Sudan)
- - - - - DINKA, SOUTHEASTERN.DIN (Sudan)
- - - - - DINKA, SOUTHWESTERN.DIK (Sudan)
- - - - Nuer (2): ATUOT.ATU (Sudan)
- - - - - NUER.NUS (Sudan)
- - - - Luo (15)

Nilo-Saharan (194)
- Songhai (4): DENDI.DEN (Niger)
- - SONGAI.SON (Mali)
- - TADAKSAHAK.DSQ (Mali)
- - ZARMA.DJE (Niger)
- Unclassified (1): SHABO.SBF (Ethiopia)

North Caucasian (34)
- North Central (3)
- - Batsi (1): BATS.BBL (Georgia)
- - Chechen-Ingush (2): CHECHEN.CJC (Russia, Europe)
- - - INGUSH.INH (Russia, Europe)
- Northeast (26)
- - Avaro-Andi-Dido (14)
- - - Andi (8): AKHVAKH.AKV (Russia, Europe)
- - - - ANDI.ANI (Russia, Europe)
- - - - BAGVALAL.KVA (Russia, Europe)
- - - - BOTLIKH.BPH (Russia, Europe)
- - - - CHAMALAL.CJI (Russia, Europe)
- - - - GHODOBERI.GDO (Russia, Europe)
- - - - KARATA.KPT (Russia, Europe)
- - - - TINDI.TIN (Russia, Europe)
- - - Avar (1): AVAR.AVR (Russia, Europe)
- - - Dido (5): BEZHTA.KAP (Russia, Europe)
- - - - DIDO.DDO (Russia, Europe)
- - - - HINUKH.GIN (Russia, Europe)
- - - - HUNZIB.HUZ (Russia, Europe)
- - - - KHVARSHI.KHV (Russia, Europe)
- - Lak-Dargwa (2): DARGWA.DAR (Russia, Europe)
- - LAK.LBE (Russia, Europe)
- - Lezgian (10): AGHUL.AGX (Russia, Europe)
- - - ARCHI.ARC (Russia, Europe)
- - - BUDUKH.BDK (Azerbaijan)
- - - KHINALUGH.KJJ (Azerbaijan)
- - - KRYTS.KRY (Azerbaijan)
- - - LEZGI.LEZ (Russia, Europe)
- - - RUTUL.RUT (Russia, Europe)
- - - TABASSARAN.TAB (Russia, Europe)
- - - TSAKHUR.TKR (Azerbaijan)
- - - UDI.UDI (Azerbaijan)
- Northwest (5)
- - Abkhaz-Abazin (2): ABAZA.ABQ (Russia, Europe)
- - - ABKHAZ.ABK (Georgia)
- - Circassian (2): ADYGHE.ADY (Russia, Europe)
- - - KABARDIAN.KAB (Russia, Europe)
- - Ubyx (1): UBYKH.UBY (Turkey)

Oto-Manguean (173)
- Amuzgoan (3): AMUZGO, GUERRERO.AMU (Mexico)
- - AMUZGO, OAXACA.AZG (Mexico)
- - AMUZGO, SANTA MARÍA IPALAPA.AZM (Mexico)
- Chiapanec-Mangue (2): CHIAPANECO.CIP (Mexico)
- - CHOROTEGA.CJR (Costa Rica)
- Chinantecan (14): CHINANTECO, CHILTEPEC.CSA (Mexico)
- - CHINANTECO, COMALTEPEC.CCO (Mexico)
- - CHINANTECO, LALANA.CNL (Mexico)
- - CHINANTECO, LEALAO.CLE (Mexico)
- - CHINANTECO, OJITLÁN.CHJ (Mexico)
- - CHINANTECO, OZUMACÍN.CHZ (Mexico)
- - CHINANTECO, PALANTLA.CPA (Mexico)
- - CHINANTECO, QUIOTEPEC.CHQ (Mexico)
- - CHINANTECO, SOCHIAPAN.CSO (Mexico)
- - CHINANTECO, TEPETOTUTLA.CNT (Mexico)
- - CHINANTECO, TEPINAPA.CTE (Mexico)
- - CHINANTECO, TLACOATZINTEPEC.CTL (Mexico)
- - CHINANTECO, USILA.CUS (Mexico)
- - CHINANTECO, VALLE NACIONAL.CHV (Mexico)
- Mixtecan (57)
- - Mixtec-Cuicatec (54)

Oto-Manguean (173)
- Otopamean (16)
- - Otomian (11)
- - - Otomi (9): OTOMÍ, TENANGO.OTN (Mexico)
- - - - OTOMÍ, TEXCATEPEC.OTX (Mexico)
- - - - OTOMÍ, TILAPA.OTL (Mexico)
- - - - OTOMÍ, WESTERN.OTQ (Mexico)
- - Pamean (2): CHICHIMECA PAME, NORTHERN.PMQ (Mexico)
- - - PAME, CENTRAL.PBS (Mexico)
- Popolocan (17)
- - Chocho-Popolocan (8)
- - - Chocho (1): CHOCHOTECO.COZ (Mexico)
- - - Popolocan (7): POPOLOCA, COYOTEPEC.PBF (Mexico)
- - - - POPOLOCA, LOS REYES MEZONTLA.PBE (Mexico)
- - - - POPOLOCA, SAN FELIPE OTLALTEPEC.POW (Mexico)
- - - - POPOLOCA, SAN JUAN ATZINGO.POE (Mexico)
- - - - POPOLOCA, SAN LUÍS TEMALACAYUCA.PPS (Mexico)
- - - - POPOLOCA, SAN MARCOS TLACOYALCO.PLS (Mexico)
- - - - POPOLOCA, SANTA INÉS AHUATEMPAN.PCA (Mexico)
- - Ixcatecan (1): IXCATECO.IXC (Mexico)
- - Mazatecan (8): MAZATECO, AYAUTLA.VMY (Mexico)
- - - MAZATECO, HUAUTLA DE JIMENEZ.MAU (Mexico)
- - - MAZATECO, MAZATLÁN.VMZ (Mexico)
- - - MAZATECO, SAN FELIPE JALAPA DE DIAZ.MAJ (Mexico)
- - - MAZATECO, SAN JERÓNIMO TECOATL.MAA (Mexico)
- - - MAZATECO, SAN JUAN CHIQUIHUITLÁN.MAQ (Mexico)
- - - MAZATECO, SAN MIGUEL SOYALTEPEC.VMP (Mexico)
- - - MAZATECO, SAN PEDRO IXCATLÁN.MAO (Mexico)
- Zapotecan (64)
- - Chatino (7): CHATINO, LACHAO-YOLOTEPEC.CLY (Mexico)
- - - CHATINO, NOPALA.CYA (Mexico)
- - - CHATINO, TATALTEPEC.CTA (Mexico)
- - - CHATINO, WEST HIGHLAND.CTP (Mexico)
- - - CHATINO, YAITEPEC.CUC (Mexico)
- - - CHATINO, ZACATEPEC.CTZ (Mexico)
- - - CHATINO, ZENZONTEPEC.CZE (Mexico)
- - Zapotec (57): ZAPOTECO, ALBARRADAS.ZAS (Mexico)
- - - ZAPOTECO, ALOAPAN.ZAQ (Mexico)
- - - ZAPOTECO, AYOQUESCO.ZAF (Mexico)
- - - ZAPOTECO, CENTRAL MIAHUATLÁN.ZAM (Mexico)
- - - ZAPOTECO, CENTRAL VILLA ALTA.ZAT (Mexico)
- - - ZAPOTECO, CHOAPAN.ZPC (Mexico)
- - - ZAPOTECO, COATECAS ALTAS.ZAP (Mexico)
- - - ZAPOTECO, EASTERN MIAHUATLÁN.ZPM (Mexico)
- - - ZAPOTECO, EASTERN POCHUTLA.ZAX (Mexico)
- - - ZAPOTECO, EASTERN SOLA DE VEGA.ZPL (Mexico)
- - - ZAPOTECO, EASTERN TLACOLULA.ZPF (Mexico)
- - - ZAPOTECO, ISTHMUS.ZAI (Mexico)
- - - ZAPOTECO, MITLA.ZAW (Mexico)
- - - ZAPOTECO, NORTH CENTRAL ZIMATLÁN.ZOO (Mexico)
- - - ZAPOTECO, NORTHEASTERN MIAHUATLÁN.ZPO (Mexico)
- - - ZAPOTECO, NORTHEASTERN YAUTEPEC.ZPJ (Mexico)
- - - ZAPOTECO, NORTHERN ISTHMUS.ZPG (Mexico)
- - - ZAPOTECO, NORTHERN VILLA ALTA.ZAR (Mexico)
- - - ZAPOTECO, NORTHWESTERN POCHUTLA.ZPX (Mexico)
- - - ZAPOTECO, NORTHWESTERN TEHUANTEPEC.ZPA (Mexico)
- - - ZAPOTECO, OZOLOTEPEC.ZAO (Mexico)
- - - ZAPOTECO, SAN AGUSTÍN MIXTEPEC.ZTM (Mexico)
- - - ZAPOTECO, SAN BALTAZAR CHICHICAPAN.ZPV (Mexico)
- - - ZAPOTECO, SAN BARTOLO YAUTEPEC.ZPB (Mexico)
- - - ZAPOTECO, SAN BARTOLOMÉ ZOOGOCHO.ZPQ (Mexico)
- - - ZAPOTECO, SAN CRISTOBAL LACHIRUAJ.ZTC (Mexico)
- - - ZAPOTECO, SAN JUAN ELOTEPEC.ZTE (Mexico)
- - - ZAPOTECO, SAN JUAN GUELAVÍA.ZAB (Mexico)
- - - ZAPOTECO, SAN LORENZO TEXMELUCAN.ZPZ (Mexico)
- - - ZAPOTECO, SAN MIGUEL TILQUIAPAN.ZTS (Mexico)
- - - ZAPOTECO, SAN PABLO GÜILÁ.ZTU (Mexico)
- - - ZAPOTECO, SANTA CATARINA ALBARRADAS.ZTN (Mexico)
- - - ZAPOTECO, SANTA CATARINA QUIERÍ.ZTQ (Mexico)

- Miwok (6)
- - Eastern (4): MIWOK, CENTRAL SIERRA.CSM (USA)
- - - - MIWOK, NORTHERN SIERRA.NSQ (USA)
- - - - MIWOK, PLAINS.PMW (USA)
- - - - MIWOK, SOUTHERN SIERRA.SKD (USA)
- - - - Western (2): MIWOK, COAST.CSI (USA)
- - - - MIWOK, LAKE.LMW (USA)
- - Wintun (Copehan) (1): WINTU.WIT (USA)
- - Yokuts (3): YOKUTS, NORTHERN FOOTHILL.YOK (USA)
- - - YOKUTS, SOUTHERN FOOTHILL.YOF (USA)
- - - YOKUTS, VALLEY.YOV (USA)
- Chinookan (2): CHINOOK.CHH (USA)
- - WASCO-WISHRAM.WAC (USA)
- Oregon Penutian (3)
- - Coos (1): COOS.COS (USA)
- - Kalapuyan (1): KALAPUYA.KAL (USA)
- - Yakonan (1): SIUSLAW.SIS (USA)
- Plateau Penutian (6)
- - Klamath-Modoc (1): KLAMATH-MODOC.KLA (USA)
- - Sahaptin (5): NEZ PERCE.NEZ (USA)
- - - TENINO.WAR (USA)
- - - UMATILLA.UMA (USA)
- - - WALLA WALLA.WAA (USA)
- - - YAKIMA.YAK (USA)
- Tsimshian (2): NASS-GITKSIAN.NCG (Canada)
- - TSIMSHIAN.TSI (Canada)

Pidgin (11)
- Amerindian (2): CHINOOK WAWA.CRW (Canada)
- - MOBILIAN.MOD (USA)
- English based (2)
- - Atlantic (1): LIBERIAN ENGLISH.LIR (Liberia)
- - Pacific (1): CHINESE PIDGIN ENGLISH.CPE (Nauru)
- French based (1): TAY BOI.TAS (Viet Nam)
- Hausa based (1): BARIKANCHI.BXO (Nigeria)
- Malay based (1): BROOME PEARLING LUGGER PIDGIN.BPL (Australia)
- Mascoian based (1): MASKOY PIDGIN.MHH (Paraguay)
- Motu based (1): MOTU, HIRI.POM (Papua New Guinea)
- Swahili based (1): SETTLA.STA (Zambia)
- Zulu based (1): FANAGOLO.FAO (South Africa)

Quechuan (47)
- Quechua I (18): QUECHUA, ANCASH, CHIQUIAN.QEC (Peru)
- - QUECHUA, ANCASH, CONCHUCOS, NORTHERN.QED (Peru)
- - QUECHUA, ANCASH, CONCHUCOS, SOUTHERN.QEH (Peru)
- - QUECHUA, ANCASH, CORONGO.QEE (Peru)
- - QUECHUA, ANCASH, HUAYLAS.QAN (Peru)
- - QUECHUA, ANCASH, SIHUAS.QES (Peru)
- - QUECHUA, HUÁNUCO, HUALLAGA.QUB (Peru)
- - QUECHUA, HUÁNUCO, HUAMALÍES-NORTHERN DOS DE MAYO.QEJ (Peru)
- - QUECHUA, HUÁNUCO, MARAÑON.QEL (Peru)
- - QUECHUA, HUÁNUCO, PANAO.QEM (Peru)
- - QUECHUA, HUÁNUCO, SOUTHERN DOS DE MAYO-MARGOS CHAULÁN.QEI (Peru)
- - QUECHUA, HUANCA, HUAYLLA.QHU (Peru)
- - QUECHUA, HUANCA, JAUJA.QHJ (Peru)
- - QUECHUA, NORTH JUNÍN.QJU (Peru)
- - QUECHUA, NORTH LIMA, CAJATAMBO.QNL (Peru)
- - QUECHUA, PASCO, SANTA ANA DE TUSI.QEF (Peru)
- - QUECHUA, PASCO-YANAHUANCA.QUR (Peru)
- - QUECHUA, SAN RAFAEL-HUARIACA.QEG (Peru)
- Quechua II (29)
- - A (4): QUECHUA, CAJAMARCA.QNT (Peru)
- - - QUECHUA, LAMBAYEQUE.QUF (Peru)
- - - QUECHUA, PACAROAS.QCP (Peru)
- - - QUECHUA, YAUYOS.QUX (Peru)
- - - B (14): INGA, JUNGLE.INJ (Colombia)
- - - INGA.INB (Colombia)
- - - QUECHUA, CHACHAPOYAS.QUK (Peru)
- - - QUECHUA, PASTAZA, SOUTHERN.QUP (Peru)

Quechuan (47)
- Quechua II (29)
- - B (14): QUECHUA, SAN MARTÍN.QSA (Peru)
- - - QUICHUA, HIGHLAND, CALDERÓN.QUD (Ecuador)
- - - QUICHUA, HIGHLAND, CAÑAR.QQC (Ecuador)
- - - QUICHUA, HIGHLAND, CHIMBORAZO.QUG (Ecuador)
- - - QUICHUA, HIGHLAND, IMBABURA.QHO (Ecuador)
- - - QUICHUA, HIGHLAND, LOJA.QQU (Ecuador)
- - - QUICHUA, HIGHLAND, TUNGURAHUA.QQS (Ecuador)
- - - QUICHUA, LOWLAND, NAPO.QLN (Ecuador)
- - - QUICHUA, LOWLAND, TENA.QUW (Ecuador)
- - - QUICHUA, PASTAZA, NORTHERN.QLB (Ecuador)
- - C (11): QUECHUA, APURIMAC.QEA (Peru)
- - - QUECHUA, AYACUCHO.QUY (Peru)
- - - QUECHUA, CHILEAN.QUE (Chile)
- - - QUECHUA, CLASSICAL.QCL (Peru)
- - - QUECHUA, COTAHUASI.QAR (Peru)
- - - QUECHUA, CUZCO.QUZ (Peru)
- - - QUECHUA, NORTH BOLIVIAN.QUL (Bolivia)
- - - QUECHUA, NORTHWEST JUJUY.QUO (Argentina)
- - - QUECHUA, PUNO.QEP (Peru)
- - - QUECHUA, SOUTH BOLIVIAN.QUH (Bolivia)
- - - QUICHUA, SANTIAGO DEL ESTERO.QUS (Argentina)

Salishan (27)
- Bella Coola (1): BELLA COOLA.BEL (Canada)
- Central Salish (13)
- - Halkomelem (1): HALKOMELEM.HUR (Canada)
- - Nooksack (1): NOOKSACK.NOK (USA)
- - Northern (3): COMOX.COO (Canada)
- - - PENTLATCH.PTW (Canada)
- - - SECHELT.SEC (Canada)
- - Squamish (1): SQUAMISH.SQU (Canada)
- - Straits (2): CLALLAM.CLM (USA)
- - - SALISH, STRAITS.STR (Canada)
- - Twana (5): LUSHOOTSEED.LUT (USA)
- - - SALISH, SOUTHERN PUGET SOUND.SLH (USA)
- - - SKAGIT.SKA (USA)
- - - SNOHOMISH.SNO (USA)
- - - TWANA.TWA (USA)
- Interior Salish (8)
- - Northern (3): LILLOOET.LIL (Canada)
- - - SHUSWAP.SHS (Canada)
- - - THOMPSON.THP (Canada)
- - Southern (5): COEUR D'ALENE.CRD (USA)
- - - COLUMBIA-WENATCHI.COL (USA)
- - - FLATHEAD-KALISPEL.FLA (USA)
- - - OKANAGAN.OKA (Canada)
- - - SPOKANE.SPO (USA)
- Tillamook (1): TILLAMOOK.TIL (USA)
- Tsamosan (4)
- - Inland (3): CHEHALIS, LOWER.CEA (USA)
- - - CHEHALIS, UPPER.CJH (USA)
- - - COWLITZ.COW (USA)
- - Maritime (1): QUINAULT.QUN (USA)

Salivan (2): PIAROA.PID (Venezuela)
- SÁLIBA.SLC (Colombia)

Sepik-Ramu (105)
- Gapun (1): TAIAP.GPN (Papua New Guinea)
- Leonhard Schultze (6)
- - Papi (2): PAPI.PPE (Papua New Guinea)
- - - SUARMIN.SEO (Papua New Guinea)
- - Walio (4): PEI.PPQ (Papua New Guinea)
- - - TUWARI.TWW (Papua New Guinea)
- - - WALIO.WLA (Papua New Guinea)
- - - YAWIYO.YBX (Papua New Guinea)
- Nor-Pondo (6)

Sepik-Ramu (105)
- Sepik (53)
- - Middle Sepik (20)
- - - Nukuma (7): APOS.APO (Papua New Guinea)
- - - - BONGOS.BXY (Papua New Guinea)
- - - - KWOMA.KMO (Papua New Guinea)
- - - - MENDE.SIM (Papua New Guinea)
- - - - WAMSAK.WBD (Papua New Guinea)
- - - - WASAMBU.WSM (Papua New Guinea)
- - - - YUBANAKOR.YUO (Papua New Guinea)
- - - Yerakai (1): YERAKAI.YRA (Papua New Guinea)
- - Ram (3): AWTUW.KMN (Papua New Guinea)
- - - KARAWA.QKR (Papua New Guinea)
- - - POUYE.BYE (Papua New Guinea)
- - Sepik Hill (14)
- - - Alamblak (2): ALAMBLAK.AMP (Papua New Guinea)
- - - - KANINGRA.KNR (Papua New Guinea)
- - - Bahinemo (7): BAHINEMO.BJH (Papua New Guinea)
- - - - BISIS.BNW (Papua New Guinea)
- - - - BITARA.BIT (Papua New Guinea)
- - - - KAPRIMAN.DJU (Papua New Guinea)
- - - - MARI.MBX (Papua New Guinea)
- - - - SUMARIUP.SIV (Papua New Guinea)
- - - - WATAKATAUI.WTK (Papua New Guinea)
- - - Sanio (5): BIKARU.BIC (Papua New Guinea)
- - - - HEWA.HAM (Papua New Guinea)
- - - - NIKSEK.GBE (Papua New Guinea)
- - - - PIAME.PIN (Papua New Guinea)
- - - - SANIYO-HIYOWE.SNY (Papua New Guinea)
- - Tama (5): KALOU.YWA (Papua New Guinea)
- - - MEHEK.NUX (Papua New Guinea)
- - - PAHI.LGT (Papua New Guinea)
- - - PASI.PSI (Papua New Guinea)
- - - YESSAN-MAYO.YSS (Papua New Guinea)
- - Upper Sepik (6)
- - - Abau (1): ABAU.AAU (Papua New Guinea)
- - - Iwam (3): AMAL.AAD (Papua New Guinea)
- - - - IWAM, SEPIK.IWS (Papua New Guinea)
- - - - IWAM.IWM (Papua New Guinea)
- - - Wogamusin (2): CHENAPIAN.CJN (Papua New Guinea)
- - - - WOGAMUSIN.WOG (Papua New Guinea)
- - Yellow River (3): AK.AKQ (Papua New Guinea)
- - - AWUN.AWW (Papua New Guinea)
- - - NAMIA.NNM (Papua New Guinea)

Sign language (2): MONASTIC SIGN LANGUAGE.MZG (Vatican State)
- PLAINS INDIAN SIGN LANGUAGE.PSD (USA)

Sino-Tibetan (360)
- Chinese (14): CHINESE, GAN.KNN (China)
- - CHINESE, HAKKA.HAK (China)
- - CHINESE, HUIZHOU.CZH (China)
- - CHINESE, JINYU.CJY (China)
- - CHINESE, MANDARIN.CHN (China)
- - CHINESE, MIN BEI.MNP (China)
- - CHINESE, MIN DONG.CDO (China)
- - CHINESE, MIN NAN.CFR (China)
- - CHINESE, MIN ZHONG.CZO (China)
- - CHINESE, PU-XIAN.CPX (China)
- - CHINESE, WU.WUU (China)
- - CHINESE, XIANG.HSN (China)
- - CHINESE, YUE.YUH (China)
- - DUNGAN.DNG (Kyrghyzstan)
- Tibeto-Burman (345)
- - Baric (102)
- - - Kachinic (2): JINGPHO.CGP (Myanmar)
- - - - TAMAN.TCL (Myanmar)
- - - Konyak-Bodo-Garo (30)
- - - - Bodo-Garo (11)

Sino-Tibetan (360)
- Tibeto-Burman (345)
- - Baric (102)
- - - Kuki-Naga (60)
- - - - Kuki-Chin (40)
- - - - - Southern (8)
- - - - - - Sho (3): CHIN, CHINBON.CNB (Myanmar)
- - - - - - - SHENDU.SHL (Bangladesh)
- - - - - - CHIN, DAAI.DAO (Myanmar)
- - - - - Unclassified (2): CHIN, CHO.CCN (Myanmar)
- - - - - - CHIN, NGAWN.CNW (Myanmar)
- - - - - Western (2): CHIRU.CDF (India)
- - - - - - KOIRENG.NKD (India)
- - - - Mikir-Meithei (2): MEITHEI.MNR (India)
- - - - - MIKIR.MJW (India)
- - - - Mru (1): MRU.MRO (Myanmar)
- - - - Naga (17): NAGA, ANGAMI.NJM (India)
- - - - - NAGA, CHOKRI.NRI (India)
- - - - - NAGA, KABUI.NKF (India)
- - - - - NAGA, KHEZHA.NKH (India)
- - - - - NAGA, KHIAMNGAN.NKY (India)
- - - - - NAGA, KHOIRAO.NKI (India)
- - - - - NAGA, LIANGMAI.NJN (India)
- - - - - NAGA, LOTHA.NJH (India)
- - - - - NAGA, MAO.NBI (India)
- - - - - NAGA, MARAM.NMA (India)
- - - - - NAGA, MZIEME.NME (India)
- - - - - NAGA, POUMEI.PMX (India)
- - - - - NAGA, PUIMEI.NPU (India)
- - - - - NAGA, RENGMA.NRE (India)
- - - - - NAGA, RONGMEI.NBU (India)
- - - - - NAGA, SEMA.NSM (India)
- - - - - NAGA, ZEME.NZM (India)
- - - Luish (1): KADO.KDV (Myanmar)
- - - Mirish (9): ADI.ADI (India)
- - - - APATANI.APT (India)
- - - - CHULIKATA.CLK (India)
- - - - DIGARO.MHU (India)
- - - - GALONG.GBH (India)
- - - - LHOBA, BOGA'ER.LHO (China)
- - - - LHOBA, YIDU.LON (India)
- - - - MIJU.MXJ (India)
- - - - NISI.DAP (India)
- - Bodic (134)
- - - Bodish (81)
- - - - Gurung (12): GHALE, KUTANG.GHT (Nepal)
- - - - - GHALE, NORTHERN.GHH (Nepal)
- - - - - GHALE, SOUTHERN.GHE (Nepal)
- - - - - GURUNG, EASTERN.GGN (Nepal)
- - - - - GURUNG.GVR (Nepal)
- - - - - MANANGBA.NMM (Nepal)
- - - - - PANCHGAUNLE.PNL (Nepal)
- - - - - TAMANG, EASTERN GORKHA.TGE (Nepal)
- - - - - TAMANG, EASTERN.TAJ (Nepal)
- - - - - TAMANG, NORTHWESTERN.TDG (Nepal)
- - - - - TAMANG, SOUTHWESTERN.TSF (Nepal)
- - - - - THAKALI.THS (Nepal)
- - - - Gyarung (3): JIARONG, EASTERN.JIR (China)
- - - - - JIARONG, NORTHERN.JYA (China)
- - - - - JIARONG, WESTERN.JIW (China)
- - - - Himalayish (18)
- - - - - Almora (4): BYANGSI.BEE (Nepal)
- - - - - - CHAUDANGSI.CDN (Nepal)
- - - - - - DARMIYA.DRD (Nepal)
- - - - - - RANGKAS.RGK (Nepal)
- - - - - Eastern (2): BARAAMU.BRD (Nepal)
- - - - - - THAMI.THF (Nepal)
- - - - - Janggali (1): JANGGALI.JNL (Nepal)
- - - - - Kanauri (11): BUNAN.BFU (India)

Sino-Tibetan (360)
- Tibeto-Burman (345)
- - Bodic (134)
- - - Bodish (81)
- - - - Himalayish (18)
- - - - - Kanauri (11): JANGSHUNG.JNA (India)
- - - - - - KANASHI.QAS (India)
- - - - - - KINNAURI, CHITKULI.CIK (India)
- - - - - - KINNAURI, LOWER.KFK (India)
- - - - - - KINNAURI, UPPER.NES (India)
- - - - - - LAHULI, CHAMBA.LAE (India)
- - - - - - LAHULI, TINAN.LBF (India)
- - - - - - SHUMCHO.SCU (India)
- - - - - - SUNAM.SSK (India)
- - - - - - TUKPA.TPQ (India)
- - - - Kaike (1): KAIKE.KZQ (Nepal)
- - - - Kusanda (1): KUSANDA.KGG (Nepal)
- - - - Monpa (1): SAGTENGPA.SGT (Bhutan)
- - - - Takpa (1): TAKPA.TKK (China)
- - - - Tibetan (36)
- - - - - Central (9): ATUENCE.ATF (China)
- - - - - - HELAMBU SHERPA.SCP (Nepal)
- - - - - - HUMLA BHOTIA.HUT (Nepal)
- - - - - - KAGATE.SYW (Nepal)
- - - - - - LHOMI.LHM (Nepal)
- - - - - - MUGU.MUK (Nepal)
- - - - - - PANANG.PCR (China)
- - - - - - TIBETAN.TIC (China)
- - - - - - TSEKU.TSK (China)
- - - - - Northern (3): AMDO.ADX (China)
- - - - - - CHONI.CDA (China)
- - - - - - KHAM.KHG (China)
- - - - - Southern (7): ADAP.ADP (Bhutan)
- - - - - - DZONGKHA.DZO (Bhutan)
- - - - - - GROMA.GRO (India)
- - - - - - JIREL.JUL (Nepal)
- - - - - - SHERPA.SCR (Nepal)
- - - - - - SIKKIMESE.SIP (India)
- - - - - - TSHALINGPA.TGF (Bhutan)
- - - - - Unclassified (12): BARAGAUNLE.BON (Nepal)
- - - - - - DOLPO.DRE (Nepal)
- - - - - - KYERUNG.KGY (Nepal)
- - - - - - LOPA.LOY (Nepal)
- - - - - - NAAPA.NAO (Nepal)
- - - - - - NUBRI.KTE (Nepal)
- - - - - - OLANGCHUNG GOLA.OLA (Nepal)
- - - - - - PUH.PUH (India)
- - - - - - SHERDUKPEN.SDP (India)
- - - - - - THUDAM BHOTE.THW (Nepal)
- - - - - - TICHURONG.TCN (Nepal)
- - - - - - TSUM.TTZ (Nepal)
- - - - - Western (5)
- - - - - - Ladakhi (2): CHANGTHANG.CNA (India)
- - - - - - - LADAKHI.LBJ (India)
- - - - - - BALTI.BFT (Pakistan)
- - - - - - PURIK.BXR (India)
- - - - - - ZANGSKARI.ZAU (India)
- - - - Tsangla (5): KEBUMTAMP.KJZ (Bhutan)
- - - - - KHENGKHA.XKF (Bhutan)
- - - - - KÜRTHÖPKHA.XKZ (Bhutan)
- - - - - SHARCHAGPAKHA.SCH (Bhutan)
- - - - - TSANGLA.TSJ (Bhutan)
- - - - Unclassified (2): DZALAKHA.DZL (Bhutan)
- - - - - NAR PHU.NPA (Nepal)
- - - - CHANTEL.CHX (Nepal)
- - - Dhimal (1): DHIMAL.DHI (Nepal)
- - - Eastern Himalayan (51)
- - - - Kiranti (50)
- - - - - Central (13)

Sino-Tibetan (360)
- Tibeto-Burman (345)
- - Burmese-Lolo (56)
- - - Burmish (13): XIANDAOHUA.XIA (China)
- - - Lolo (43)
- - - - Minchia (1): BAI.PIQ (China)
- - - - Northern (12)
- - - - - Lisu (2): LIPO.TKL (China)
- - - - - - LISU.LIS (China)
- - - - - Unclassified (3): KADUO.KTP (Laos)
- - - - - - NAXI.NBF (China)
- - - - - - SAMEI.SMH (China)
- - - - - Yi (7): NAMUYI.NMY (China)
- - - - - - YI, CENTRAL.YIC (China)
- - - - - - YI, GUIZHOU.YIG (China)
- - - - - - YI, SICHUAN.III (China)
- - - - - - YI, SOUTHEASTERN.YIE (China)
- - - - - - YI, WESTERN.YIW (China)
- - - - - - YI, YUNNAN.NOS (China)
- - - - Residual Lolo (6): HORPA.HRP (Myanmar)
- - - - HSIFAN.HSI (Myanmar)
- - - - MANYAK.YMY (Myanmar)
- - - - MENIA.QME (Myanmar)
- - - - MULI.QMU (Myanmar)
- - - - UGONG.UGO (Thailand)
- - - - Southern (17)
- - - - Akha (9)
- - - - - Hani (4)
- - - - - - Bi-Ka (1): BIYO.BYO (China)
- - - - - - Ha-Ya (2): AKHA.AKA (Myanmar)
- - - - - - - HANI.HNI (China)
- - - - - - Hao-Bai (1): HONI.HOW (China)
- - - - - Lahu (2): LAHU SHI.KDS (Myanmar)
- - - - - - LAHU.LAH (China)
- - - - - MAHEI.MJA (Myanmar)
- - - - - PHANA'.PHN (Laos)
- - - - - SANSU.SCA (Myanmar)
- - - - Phunoi (5): BISU.BII (China)
- - - - - MPI.MPZ (Thailand)
- - - - - PHUNOI.PHO (Laos)
- - - - - PHUNOI.PHO (Viet Nam)
- - - - - PYEN.PYY (Myanmar)
- - - - JINUO, BUYUAN.JIYY (China)
- - - - JINUO, YOULE.JIU (China)
- - - - SILA.SLT (Laos)
- - - - Unclassified (7): BELA.BEQ (China)
- - - - LAOPANG.LBG (Myanmar)
- - - - LOPI.LOV (Myanmar)
- - - - NUSU.NUF (China)
- - - - TUJIA, NORTHERN.TJI (China)
- - - - TUJIA, SOUTHERN.TJS (China)
- - - - ZAUZOU.ZAL (China)
- - Karen (21)
- - - Pho (6)
- - - Pa'o (1): KAREN, PA'O.BLK (Myanmar)
- - - Pho-Phlon (5): KAREN, NORTHERN PWO.KJT (Thailand)
- - - - KAREN, PWO KANCHANA BURI.KJP (Thailand)
- - - - KAREN, PWO OMKOI.PWW (Thailand)
- - - - KAREN, PWO RATCHABURI.KJF (Thailand)
- - - - KAREN, PWO.PWO (Myanmar)
- - - Sgaw-Bghai (11)
- - - Bghai (5)
- - - - Eastern (2): KAREN, LAHTA.KVT (Myanmar)
- - - - - KAREN, PADAUNG.PDU (Myanmar)
- - - - Unclassified (2): KAREN, BWE.BWE (Myanmar)
- - - - - KAREN, GEKO.GHK (Myanmar)
- - - - Western (1): KAREN, GEBA.KVQ (Myanmar)
- - - Brek (1): KAREN, BREK.KVL (Myanmar)
- - - Kayah (3): KAREN, YINBAW.KVU (Myanmar)

Sino-Tibetan (360)
- Tibeto-Burman (345)
- - Karen (21)
- - - Sgaw-Bghai (11)
- - - - Kayah (3): KAYAH, EASTERN.EKY (Thailand)
- - - - - KAYAH, WESTERN.KYU (Myanmar)
- - - - Sgaw (2): KAREN, PAKU.KPP (Myanmar)
- - - - - KAREN, S'GAW.KSW (Myanmar)
- - - Unclassified (4): KAREN, MANUMANAW.KXF (Myanmar)
- - - - KAREN, YINTALE.KVY (Myanmar)
- - - - KAREN, ZAYEIN.KXK (Myanmar)
- - - - WEWAW.WEA (Myanmar)
- - Nungish (5): DRUNG.DUU (China)
- - - LAMA.LAY (Myanmar)
- - - NORRA.NOR (Myanmar)
- - - NUNG.NUN (Myanmar)
- - - RAWANG.RAW (Myanmar)
- - Qiang (10): QIANG, DZORGAI.DZI (China)
- - - QIANG, KORTSE.KBG (China)
- - - QIANG, LOFUCHAI.LFU (China)
- - - QIANG, NORTHERN.CNG (China)
- - - QIANG, PINGFANG.PFG (China)
- - - QIANG, SOUTHERN.QMR (China)
- - - QIANG, THOCHU.TCJ (China)
- - - QIANG, WAGSOD.WGS (China)
- - - QUEYU.QEY (China)
- - - ZHABA.ZHA (China)
- - Unclassified (17): ANU.ANL (Myanmar)
- - - AYI.AYX (China)
- - - DARANG DENG.DAT (China)
- - - ERGONG.ERO (China)
- - - ERSU.ERS (China)
- - - GEMAN DENG.GEN (China)
- - - GUIQIONG.GQI (China)
- - - LUI.LBA (Myanmar)
- - - MOPHA.MPW (Myanmar)
- - - MUYA.MVM (China)
- - - PALU.PBZ (Myanmar)
- - - PAO.PPA (India)
- - - PUMI, NORTHERN.PMI (China)
- - - PUMI, SOUTHERN.PUS (China)
- - - SHIXING.SXG (China)
- - - SULUNG.SUV (India)
- - - WELAUNG.WEL (Myanmar)
- Unclassified (1): WUTUNHUA.WUH (China)

Siouan (17)
- Catawba (1): CATAWBA.CHC (USA)
- Siouan Proper (16)
- - Central (10)
- - - Mandan (1): MANDAN.MHQ (USA)
- - - Mississippi Valley (9)
- - - - Chiwere (1): IOWA-OTO.IOW (USA)
- - - - Dakota (3): ASSINIBOINE.ASB (Canada)
- - - - - LAKOTA.LKT (USA)
- - - - - STONEY.STO (Canada)
- - - - Dhegiha (4): KANSA.KAA (USA)
- - - - - OMAHA-PONCA.OMA (USA)
- - - - - OSAGE.OSA (USA)
- - - - - QUAPAW.QUA (USA)
- - - - Winnebago (1): HOCÁK.WIN (USA)
- - Mississippi Valley (1)
- - Dakota (1): DAKOTA.DHG (USA)
- - Missouri Valley (2): CROW.CRO (USA)
- - HIDATSA.HID (USA)
- - Southeastern (3)
- - Biloxi-Ofo (2): BILOXI.BLL (USA)
- - - OFO.OFO (USA)
- - Tutelo (1): TUTELO.TTA (USA)

Sko (8)
- Krisa (4): KRISA.KRO (Papua New Guinea)
- - PUARI.PUX (Papua New Guinea)
- - RAWO.RWA (Papua New Guinea)
- - WARAPU.WRA (Papua New Guinea)
- Vanimo (4): SANGKE.SKG (Indonesia, Irian Jaya)
- - SKO.SKV (Indonesia, Irian Jaya)
- - VANIMO.VAM (Papua New Guinea)
- - WUTUNG.WUT (Papua New Guinea)

South Caucasian (5)
- Georgian (2): GEORGIAN.GEO (Georgia)
- - JUDEO-GEORGIAN.JGE (Israel)
- Svan (1): SVAN.SVA (Georgia)
- Zan (2): LAZ.LZZ (Turkey)
- - MINGRELIAN.XMF (Georgia)

Subtiaba-Tlapanec (4): SUBTIABA.SUT (Nicaragua)
- TLAPANECO, ACATEPEC.TPX (Mexico)
- TLAPANECO, AZOYÚ.TPC (Mexico)
- TLAPANECO, MALINALTEPEC.TLL (Mexico)

Tacanan (6)
- Araona-Tacana (5)
- - Araona (1): ARAONA.ARO (Bolivia)
- - Cavinena-Tacana (4)
- - - Cavinena (1): CAVINEÑA.CAV (Bolivia)
- - - Tacana Proper (3): REYESANO.REY (Bolivia)
- - - - TACANA.TNA (Bolivia)
- - - - TOROMONO.TNO (Bolivia)
- Tiatinagua (1): ESE EJJA.ESE (Bolivia)

Torricelli (48)
- Kombio-Arapesh (9)
- - Arapesh (3): ARAPESH, BUMBITA.AON (Papua New Guinea)
- - - BUKIYIP.APE (Papua New Guinea)
- - - MUFIAN.AOJ (Papua New Guinea)
- - Kombio (6): ARUEK.AUR (Papua New Guinea)
- - - EITIEP.EIT (Papua New Guinea)
- - - KOMBIO.KOK (Papua New Guinea)
- - - TORRICELLI.TEI (Papua New Guinea)
- - - WOM.WMO (Papua New Guinea)
- - - YAMBES.YMB (Papua New Guinea)
- Maimai (6)
- - Beli (1): BELI.BEY (Papua New Guinea)
- - Laeko-Libuat (1): LAEKO-LIBUAT.LKL (Papua New Guinea)
- - Maimai Proper (3): SILIPUT.MKC (Papua New Guinea)
- - - WANIB.AUK (Papua New Guinea)
- - - YAHANG.RHP (Papua New Guinea)
- - Wiaki (1): WIAKI.WII (Papua New Guinea)
- Marienberg (7): BUNA.BVN (Papua New Guinea)
- - BUNGAIN.BUT (Papua New Guinea)
- - ELEPI.ELE (Papua New Guinea)
- - KAMASAU.KMS (Papua New Guinea)
- - MANDI.TUA (Papua New Guinea)
- - MUNIWARA.MWB (Papua New Guinea)
- - URIMO.URX (Papua New Guinea)
- Monumbo (2): LILAU.LLL (Papua New Guinea)
- - MONUMBO.MXK (Papua New Guinea)
- Urim (1): URIM.URI (Papua New Guinea)
- Wapei-Palei (20)
- - Palei (7): AGI.AIF (Papua New Guinea)
- - - AIKU.MZF (Papua New Guinea)
- - - ALATIL.ALX (Papua New Guinea)
- - - ARUOP.LSR (Papua New Guinea)
- - - BRAGAT.AOF (Papua New Guinea)
- - - NABI.MTY (Papua New Guinea)
- - - WANAP.WNP (Papua New Guinea)
- - Urat (1): URAT.URT (Papua New Guinea)

Torricelli (48)
- Wapei-Palei (20)
- - Wapei (12): AU.AVT (Papua New Guinea)
- - - DIA.DIA (Papua New Guinea)
- - - ELKEI.ELK (Papua New Guinea)
- - - GNAU.GNU (Papua New Guinea)
- - - NINGIL.NIZ (Papua New Guinea)
- - - OLO.ONG (Papua New Guinea)
- - - SINAGEN.SIU (Papua New Guinea)
- - - VALMAN.VAN (Papua New Guinea)
- - - YAPUNDA.YEV (Papua New Guinea)
- - - YAU.YYU (Papua New Guinea)
- - - YIL.YLL (Papua New Guinea)
- - - YIS.YIS (Papua New Guinea)
- West Wapei (3): AUNALEI.AUN (Papua New Guinea)
- - SETA.STF (Papua New Guinea)
- - SETI.SBI (Papua New Guinea)

Totonacan (11)
- Tepehua (3): TEPEHUA, HUEHUETLA.TEE (Mexico)
- - TEPEHUA, PISA FLORES.TPP (Mexico)
- - TEPEHUA, TLACHICHILCO.TPT (Mexico)
- Totonac (8): TOTONACA, COYUTLA.TOC (Mexico)
- - TOTONACA, FILOMENO MATA-COAHUITLÁN.TLP (Mexico)
- - TOTONACA, NORTHERN.TOO (Mexico)
- - TOTONACA, OZUMATLÁN.TQT (Mexico)
- - TOTONACA, PAPANTLA.TOP (Mexico)
- - TOTONACA, PATLA.TOT (Mexico)
- - TOTONACA, SIERRA.TOS (Mexico)
- - TOTONACA, YECUATLA.TLC (Mexico)

Trans-New Guinea (539)
- Eleman (7)
- - Eleman Proper (5)
- - - Eastern (2): TOARIPI.TPI (Papua New Guinea)
- - - - UARIPI.UAR (Papua New Guinea)
- - - Western (3): KEURU.QQK (Papua New Guinea)
- - - - OPAO.OPO (Papua New Guinea)
- - - - OROKOLO.ORO (Papua New Guinea)
- - Purari (1): PURARI.IAR (Papua New Guinea)
- - Tate (1): KAKI AE.TBD (Papua New Guinea)
- Inland Gulf (4)
- - Ipiko (1): IPIKO.IPK (Papua New Guinea)
- - Minanibai (3): KARAMI.XAR (Papua New Guinea)
- - - MINANIBAI.MCV (Papua New Guinea)
- - - TAO-SUAMATO.TSX (Papua New Guinea)
- Kaure (4)
- - Kaure Proper (3): KAURE.BPP (Indonesia, Irian Jaya)
- - - KOSADLE.KIQ (Indonesia, Irian Jaya)
- - - NARAU.NXU (Indonesia, Irian Jaya)
- - KAPORI.KHP (Indonesia, Irian Jaya)
- Kolopom (3): KIMAGHAMA.KIG (Indonesia, Irian Jaya)
- - NDOM.NQM (Indonesia, Irian Jaya)
- - RIANTANA.RAN (Indonesia, Irian Jaya)
- Madang-Adelbert Range (102)
- - Adelbert Range (44)
- - - Brahman (4): BIYOM.BPM (Papua New Guinea)
- - - - FAITA.FAT (Papua New Guinea)
- - - - ISABI.ISA (Papua New Guinea)
- - - - TAUYA.TYA (Papua New Guinea)
- - - Josephstaal-Wanang (12)
- - - - Josephstaal (7)
- - - - - Osum (1): UTARMBUNG.OMO (Papua New Guinea)
- - - - - Pomoikan (3): ANAM.PDA (Papua New Guinea)
- - - - - - ANAMGURA.IMI (Papua New Guinea)
- - - - - - MORESADA.MSX (Papua New Guinea)
- - - - - Sikan (2): MUM.KQA (Papua New Guinea)
- - - - - - SILEIBI.SBQ (Papua New Guinea)
- - - - - Wadaginam (1): WADAGINAM.WDG (Papua New Guinea)

Trans-New Guinea (539)
- Main Section (300)
- - Central and Western (254)
- - - Dani-Kwerba (21)
- - - - Southern (13)
- - - - - Ngalik-Nduga (5): NDUGA.NDX (Indonesia, Irian Jaya)
- - - - - - SILIMO.WUL (Indonesia, Irian Jaya)
- - - - - - YALI, ANGGURUK.YLI (Indonesia, Irian Jaya)
- - - - - - YALI, NINIA.NLK (Indonesia, Irian Jaya)
- - - - - - YALI, PASS VALLEY.YAC (Indonesia, Irian Jaya)
- - - - - Wano (1): WANO.WNO (Indonesia, Irian Jaya)
- - - Dem (1): DEM.DEM (Indonesia, Irian Jaya)
- - - East New Guinea Highlands (65)
- - - - Central (18)
- - - - - Chimbu (7): CHUAVE.CJV (Papua New Guinea)
- - - - - - DOM.DOA (Papua New Guinea)
- - - - - - GOLIN.GVF (Papua New Guinea)
- - - - - - KUMAN.KUE (Papua New Guinea)
- - - - - - NOMANE.NOF (Papua New Guinea)
- - - - - - SALT-YUI.SLL (Papua New Guinea)
- - - - - - SINASINA.SST (Papua New Guinea)
- - - - - Hagen (4)
- - - - - - Kaugel (3): IMBONGU.IMO (Papua New Guinea)
- - - - - - - MBO-UNG.MUX (Papua New Guinea)
- - - - - - - UMBU-UNGU.UMB (Papua New Guinea)
- - - - - - MEDLPA.MED (Papua New Guinea)
- - - - - Jimi (3): KANDAWO.GAM (Papua New Guinea)
- - - - - - MARING.MBW (Papua New Guinea)
- - - - - - NARAK.NAC (Papua New Guinea)
- - - - - Wahgi (4): KUMAI.KMI (Papua New Guinea)
- - - - - - NEMBI.NMX (Papua New Guinea)
- - - - - - NII.NII (Papua New Guinea)
- - - - - - WAHGI.WAK (Papua New Guinea)
- - - - East-Central (14)
- - - - - Fore (2): FORE.FOR (Papua New Guinea)
- - - - - - GIMI.GIM (Papua New Guinea)
- - - - - Gahuku-Benabena (4): ALEKANO.GAH (Papua New Guinea)
- - - - - - BENABENA.BEF (Papua New Guinea)
- - - - - - DANO.ASO (Papua New Guinea)
- - - - - - TOKANO.ZUH (Papua New Guinea)
- - - - - Gende (1): GENDE.GAF (Papua New Guinea)
- - - - - Kamano-Yagaria (5): INOKE-YATE.INO (Papua New Guinea)
- - - - - - KAMANO.KBQ (Papua New Guinea)
- - - - - - KANITE.KMU (Papua New Guinea)
- - - - - - KEYAGANA.KYG (Papua New Guinea)
- - - - - - YAGARIA.YGR (Papua New Guinea)
- - - - - Siane (2): SIANE.SNP (Papua New Guinea)
- - - - - - YAWEYUHA.YBY (Papua New Guinea)
- - - - Eastern (13)
- - - - - Gadsup-Auyana-Awa (7): AGARABI.AGD (Papua New Guinea)
- - - - - - AWA.AWB (Papua New Guinea)
- - - - - - AWIYAANA.AUY (Papua New Guinea)
- - - - - - GADSUP.GAJ (Papua New Guinea)
- - - - - - KOSENA.KZE (Papua New Guinea)
- - - - - - ONTENU.ONT (Papua New Guinea)
- - - - - - USARUFA.USA (Papua New Guinea)
- - - - - Kambaira (1): KAMBAIRA.KYY (Papua New Guinea)
- - - - - Owenia (1): OWENIA.WSR (Papua New Guinea)
- - - - - Tairora (4): BINUMARIEN.BJR (Papua New Guinea)
- - - - - - OMWUNRA-TOGURA.OMW (Papua New Guinea)
- - - - - - TAIRORA.TBG (Papua New Guinea)
- - - - - - WAFFA.WAJ (Papua New Guinea)
- - - - Kalam (4)
- - - - - Gants (1): GANTS.GAO (Papua New Guinea)
- - - - - Kalam-Kobon (2): KALAM.KMH (Papua New Guinea)
- - - - - - KOBON.KPW (Papua New Guinea)
- - - - - Unclassified (1): TAI.TAW (Papua New Guinea)
- - - - Kenati (1): KENATI.GAT (Papua New Guinea)
- - - - West-Central (14)

Trans-New Guinea (539)
- Main Section (300)
- - Central and Western (254)
- - - Huon-Finisterre (62)
- - - - Huon (21)
- - - - - Eastern (8): MIGABAC.MPP (Papua New Guinea)
- - - - - - MOMARE.MSZ (Papua New Guinea)
- - - - - - SENE.SEJ (Papua New Guinea)
- - - - - Kovai (1): KOVAI.KQB (Papua New Guinea)
- - - - - Western (12): BURUM-MINDIK.BMU (Papua New Guinea)
- - - - - - KINALAKNA.KCO (Papua New Guinea)
- - - - - - KOMBA.KPF (Papua New Guinea)
- - - - - - KUMUKIO.KUO (Papua New Guinea)
- - - - - - MESEM.MCI (Papua New Guinea)
- - - - - - NABAK.NAF (Papua New Guinea)
- - - - - - NOMU.NOH (Papua New Guinea)
- - - - - - ONO.ONS (Papua New Guinea)
- - - - - - SELEPET.SEL (Papua New Guinea)
- - - - - - SIALUM.SLW (Papua New Guinea)
- - - - - - TIMBE.TIM (Papua New Guinea)
- - - - - - TOBO.TBV (Papua New Guinea)
- - - Kayagar (3): ATOHWAIM.AQM (Indonesia, Irian Jaya)
- - - - KAYGIR.KYT (Indonesia, Irian Jaya)
- - - - TAMAGARIO.TCG (Indonesia, Irian Jaya)
- - - Mairasi-Tanamerah (4)
- - - - Mairasi (3): MAIRASI.FRY (Indonesia, Irian Jaya)
- - - - - MER.MNU (Indonesia, Irian Jaya)
- - - - - SEMIMI.ETZ (Indonesia, Irian Jaya)
- - - - Tanamerah (1): TANAHMERAH.TCM (Indonesia, Irian Jaya)
- - - Marind (6)
- - - - Boazi (2): BOAZI.KVG (Papua New Guinea)
- - - - - ZIMAKANI.ZIK (Papua New Guinea)
- - - - Marind Proper (2): MARIND, BIAN.BPV (Indonesia, Irian Jaya)
- - - - - MARIND.MRZ (Indonesia, Irian Jaya)
- - - - Yaqay (2): WARKAY-BIPIM.BGV (Indonesia, Irian Jaya)
- - - - - YAQAY.JAQ (Indonesia, Irian Jaya)
- - - Mor (1): MOR.MOQ (Indonesia, Irian Jaya)
- - - Sentani (4)
- - - - Sentani Proper (3): NAFRI.NXX (Indonesia, Irian Jaya)
- - - - - SENTANI.SET (Indonesia, Irian Jaya)
- - - - - TABLA.TNM (Indonesia, Irian Jaya)
- - - - DEMTA.DMY (Indonesia, Irian Jaya)
- - - West Bomberai (3)
- - - - Karas (1): KARAS.KGV (Indonesia, Irian Jaya)
- - - - West Bomberai Proper (2): BAHAM.BDW (Indonesia, Irian Jaya)
- - - - - IHA.IHP (Indonesia, Irian Jaya)
- - - Wissel Lakes-Kemandoga (6)
- - - - Ekari-Wolani-Moni (5): AUYE.AUU (Indonesia, Irian Jaya)
- - - - - DAO.DAZ (Indonesia, Irian Jaya)
- - - - - EKARI.EKG (Indonesia, Irian Jaya)
- - - - - MONI.MNZ (Indonesia, Irian Jaya)
- - - - - WOLANI.WOD (Indonesia, Irian Jaya)
- - - - Uhunduni (1): DAMAL.UHN (Indonesia, Irian Jaya)
- - Eastern (46)
- - - Binanderean (10)
- - - - Binanderean Proper (9): BARUGA.BBB (Papua New Guinea)
- - - - - BINANDERE.BHG (Papua New Guinea)
- - - - - EWAGE-NOTU.NOU (Papua New Guinea)
- - - - - GAINA.GCN (Papua New Guinea)
- - - - - KORAFE.KPR (Papua New Guinea)
- - - - - OROKAIVA.ORK (Papua New Guinea)
- - - - - SUENA.SUE (Papua New Guinea)
- - - - - YEKORA.YKR (Papua New Guinea)
- - - - - ZIA.ZIA (Papua New Guinea)
- - - - Guhu-Samane (1): GUHU-SAMANE.GHS (Papua New Guinea)
- - - Central and Southeastern (36)
- - - - Dagan (9): DAGA.DGZ (Papua New Guinea)
- - - - - GINUMAN.GNM (Papua New Guinea)
- - - - - JIMAJIMA.JMA (Papua New Guinea)

Trans-New Guinea (539)
- Trans-Fly-Bulaka River (32)
- - Bulaka River (2): MAKLEW.MGF (Indonesia, Irian Jaya)
- - - YELMEK.JEL (Indonesia, Irian Jaya)
- - Trans-Fly (30)
- - - Eastern Trans-Fly (4): BINE.ORM (Papua New Guinea)
- - - - GIDRA.GDR (Papua New Guinea)
- - - - GIZRA.TOF (Papua New Guinea)
- - - - MERIAM.ULK (Australia)
- - - Kiwaian (6): BAMU.BCF (Papua New Guinea)
- - - - KEREWO.KXZ (Papua New Guinea)
- - - - KIWAI, NORTHEAST.KIW (Papua New Guinea)
- - - - KIWAI, SOUTHERN.KJD (Papua New Guinea)
- - - - KIWAI, WABUDA.KMX (Papua New Guinea)
- - - - MORIGI.MDB (Papua New Guinea)
- - - Moraori (1): MORAORI.MOK (Indonesia, Irian Jaya)
- - - Morehead and Upper Maro Rivers (11)
- - - - Nambu (3): MARI.MXW (Papua New Guinea)
- - - - - NAMBU.NCM (Papua New Guinea)
- - - - - TAIS.TST (Papua New Guinea)
- - - - Tonda (7): ARA.TCI (Papua New Guinea)
- - - - - ARAMBA.STK (Papua New Guinea)
- - - - - BLAFE.IND (Papua New Guinea)
- - - - - GUNTAI.GNT (Papua New Guinea)
- - - - - KANUM.KCD (Papua New Guinea)
- - - - - KUNJA.PEP (Papua New Guinea)
- - - - - REMA.BOW (Papua New Guinea)
- - - - Yey (1): YEI.JEI (Indonesia, Irian Jaya)
- - - Pahoturi (2): AGOB.KIT (Papua New Guinea)
- - - - IDI.IDI (Papua New Guinea)
- - - Tirio (5): ATURU.AUP (Papua New Guinea)
- - - - BARAMU.BMZ (Papua New Guinea)
- - - - LEWADA-DEWARA.LWD (Papua New Guinea)
- - - - MUTUM.MCC (Papua New Guinea)
- - - - TIRIO.TCR (Papua New Guinea)
- - Waia (1): TABO.KNV (Papua New Guinea)
- Turama-Kikorian (3)
- - Kairi (1): RUMU.KLQ (Papua New Guinea)
- - Turama-Omatian (2): IKOBI-MENA.MEB (Papua New Guinea)
- - - OMATI.MGX (Papua New Guinea)
- Usku (1): USKU.ULF (Indonesia, Irian Jaya)

Tucanoan (26)
- Central Tucanoan (1): CUBEO.CUB (Colombia)
- Eastern Tucanoan (16)
- - Central (11)
- - - Bara (4): POKANGÁ.POK (Brazil)
- - - - TUYUCA.TUE (Colombia)
- - - - WAIMAHA.BAO (Colombia)
- - - - YURUTI.YUI (Colombia)
- - - Desano (2): DESANO.DES (Brazil)
- - - - SIRIANO.SRI (Colombia)
- - - Southern (3): BARASANA.BSN (Colombia)
- - - - JEPA-MATSI.JEP (Brazil)
- - - - MACUNA.MYY (Colombia)
- - - Tatuyo (2): CARAPANA.CBC (Colombia)
- - - - TATUYO.TAV (Colombia)
- - Northern (4): ARAPASO.ARJ (Brazil)
- - - GUANANO.GVC (Brazil)
- - - PIRATAPUYO.PIR (Brazil)
- - - TUCANO.TUO (Brazil)
- - Unclassified (1): YAHUNA.YNU (Colombia)
- Miriti (1): MIRITI.MMV (Brazil)
- Western Tucanoan (8)
- - Northern (6)
- - - Coreguaje (1): KOREGUAJE.COE (Colombia)
- - - Siona-Secoya (3): MACAGUAJE.MCL (Colombia)
- - - - SECOYA.SEY (Ecuador)
- - - - SIONA.SIN (Colombia)

Tucanoan (26)
- Western Tucanoan (8)
- - Northern (6)
- - - Tama (1): TAMA.TEN (Colombia)
- - - Tetete (1): TETETE.TEB (Ecuador)
- - Southern (1): OREJÓN.ORE (Peru)
- - Tanimuca (1): TANIMUCA-RETUARÃ.TNC (Colombia)

Tupi (70)
- Arikem (1): KARITIÂNA.KTN (Brazil)
- Aweti (1): AWETÍ.AWE (Brazil)
- Mawe-Satere (1): SATERÉ-MAWÉ.MAV (Brazil)
- Monde (6): ARUÁ.ARX (Brazil)
- - CINTA LARGA.CIN (Brazil)
- - GAVIÃO DO JIPARANÁ.GVO (Brazil)
- - MEKEM.XME (Brazil)
- - MONDÉ.MND (Brazil)
- - SURUÍ.SRU (Brazil)
- Munduruku (2): KURUÁYA.KYR (Brazil)
- - MUNDURUKÚ.MYU (Brazil)
- Purubora (1): PURUBORÁ.PUR (Brazil)
- Ramarama (2): ARÁRA, RONDÔNIA.ARR (Brazil)
- - ITOGAPÚK.ITG (Brazil)
- Tupari (4): KANOÉ.KXO (Brazil)
- - MAKURÁP.MAG (Brazil)
- - TUPARÍ.TUP (Brazil)
- - WAYORÓ.WYR (Brazil)
- Tupi-Guarani (49)
- - Guarani (I) (10): ACHÉ.GUQ (Paraguay)
- - - CHIRIGUANO.GUI (Bolivia)
- - - CHIRIPÁ.NHD (Paraguay)
- - - GUARANÍ, BOLIVIAN, WESTERN.GNW (Bolivia)
- - - GUARANÍ, MBYÁ.GUN (Paraguay)
- - - GUARANÍ, PARAGUAYAN.GUG (Paraguay)
- - - KAIWÁ.KGK (Brazil)
- - - PAI TAVYTERA.PTA (Paraguay)
- - - TAPIETÉ.TAI (Paraguay)
- - - XETÁ.XET (Brazil)
- - Guarayu-Siriono-Jora (II) (3): GUARAYU.GYR (Bolivia)
- - - JORÁ.JOR (Bolivia)
- - - SIRIONÓ.SRQ (Bolivia)
- - Kamayura (VII) (1): KAMAYURÁ.KAY (Brazil)
- - Kawahib (VI) (9): AMONDAWA.ADW (Brazil)
- - - APIACÁ.API (Brazil)
- - - JÚMA.JUA (Brazil)
- - - MOREREBI.XMO (Brazil)
- - - PARANAWÁT.PAF (Brazil)
- - - TENHARIM.PAH (Brazil)
- - - TUKUMANFÉD.TKF (Brazil)
- - - URU-EU-UAU-UAU.URZ (Brazil)
- - - WIRAFÉD.WIR (Brazil)
- - Kayabi-Arawete (V) (3): ARAWETÉ.AWT (Brazil)
- - - ASURINÍ, XINGÚ.ASN (Brazil)
- - - KAYABÍ.KYZ (Brazil)
- - Oyampi (VIII) (8): AMANAYÉ.AMA (Brazil)
- - - ANAMBÉ.AAN (Brazil)
- - - EMERILLON.EME (French Guiana)
- - - GUAJÁ.GUJ (Brazil)
- - - POTURU.PTO (Brazil)
- - - URUBÚ-KAAPOR.URB (Brazil)
- - - WAYAMPI, AMAPARI.OYM (Brazil)
- - - WAYAMPI, OIAPOQUE.OYA (French Guiana)
- - Pauserna (1): PAUSERNA.PSM (Bolivia)
- - Tenetehara (IV) (8): ASURINÍ.ASU (Brazil)
- - - AVÁ-CANOEIRO.AVV (Brazil)
- - - GUAJAJÁRA.GUB (Brazil)
- - - PARAKANÃ.PAK (Brazil)
- - - SURUÍ DO PARÁ.MDZ (Brazil)
- - - TAPIRAPÉ.TAF (Brazil)

Tupi (70)
- Tupi-Guarani (49)
- - Tenetehara (IV) (8): TEMBÉ.TEM (Brazil)
- - - TURIWÁRA.TWT (Brazil)
- - Tupi (III) (6): COCAMA-COCAMILLA.COD (Peru)
- - - NHENGATU.YRL (Brazil)
- - - OMAGUA.OMG (Peru)
- - - POTIGUÁRA.POG (Brazil)
- - - TUPINAMBÁ.TPN (Brazil)
- - - TUPINIKIN.TPK (Brazil)
- Unclassified (1): YUQUI.YUQ (Bolivia)
- Yuruna (2)
- - Manitswa (1): MANITSAUÁ.MSP (Brazil)
- - Yuruna-Chipaya (1): JURÚNA.JUR (Brazil)

Unclassified (114): AARIYA.AAR (India)
- ABISHIRA.ASH (Peru)
- AGAVOTAGUERRA.AVO (Brazil)
- AGUANO.AGA (Peru)
- AMBO.AMB (Nigeria)
- AMERAX.AEX (USA)
- AMIKOANA.AKN (Brazil)
- ANDH.ANR (India)
- ANLO.AOL (Togo)
- ARÁRA, ACRE.AXA (Brazil)
- ARÁRA, MATO GROSSO.AXG (Brazil)
- ARAKH.AAH (India)
- BALENQUE.BQV (Equatorial Guinea)
- BASO.BSA (Indonesia, Irian Jaya)
- BATHUDI.BGH (India)
- BEDIA.BXD (India)
- BETAF.BFE (Indonesia, Irian Jaya)
- BETE.BYF (Nigeria)
- BHATOLA.BTL (India)
- BHIM.BMM (India)
- BHOTTARA.BHR (India)
- BUNG.BQD (Cameroon)
- CAGUA.CBH (Colombia)
- CALLAWALLA.CAW (Bolivia)
- CANICHANA.CAZ (Bolivia)
- CARABAYO.CBY (Colombia)
- CHAK.CKH (Myanmar)
- CHERO.CRR (India)
- CHIPIAJES.CBE (Colombia)
- CHOLON.CHT (Peru)
- COXIMA.KOX (Colombia)
- DAL.DLL (India)
- GIBANAWA.GIB (Nigeria)
- HIBITO.HIB (Peru)
- HIMARIMÃ.HIR (Brazil)
- HWLA.HWL (Togo)
- IAPAMA.IAP (Brazil)
- IMERAGUEN.IME (Mauritania)
- KAIMBÉ.QKQ (Brazil)
- KAMBA.QKZ (Brazil)
- KAMBIWÁ.QKH (Brazil)
- KAPINAWÁ.QKP (Brazil)
- KARA.KAH (Central African Republic)
- KARAHAWYANA.XKH (Brazil)
- KARIPÚNA.KGM (Brazil)
- KARIRI-XOCÓ.KZW (Brazil)
- KEMBRA.XKW (Indonesia, Irian Jaya)
- KIRIRÍ-XOKÓ.XOO (Brazil)
- KOHOROXITARI.KOB (Brazil)
- KOL.KFO (India)
- KOLAI.KKX (India)
- KOROBORÉ.KBI (Burkina Faso)
- KORUBO.QKF (Brazil)
- KUJARGE.VKJ (Chad)

Unclassified (114): KUMBERAHA.XKS (Indonesia, Sulawesi)
- KUNZA.KUZ (Chile)
- KWAVI.CKG (Tanzania)
- LAAL.GDM (Chad)
- LECO.LEC (Bolivia)
- LENCA.LEN (Honduras)
- LEPKI.LPE (Indonesia, Irian Jaya)
- LUFU.LDQ (Nigeria)
- LUO.LUW (Cameroon)
- MAJHWAR.MMJ (India)
- MALAKHEL.MLD (Afghanistan)
- MATIA.MMC (India)
- MAWA.WMA (Nigeria)
- MIARRÃ.XMI (Brazil)
- MINDAT.VMT (Myanmar)
- MONIMBO.MOL (Nicaragua)
- MOVIMA.MZP (Bolivia)
- MUKHA-DORA.MMK (India)
- MULIA.MUC (India)
- MUNICHE.MYR (Peru)
- MURKIM.RMH (Indonesia, Irian Jaya)
- MUTÚS.MUF (Venezuela)
- NATAGAIMAS.NTS (Colombia)
- NEMADI.NED (Mauritania)
- NUKAK MAKÚ.MBR (Colombia)
- PANIKA.PNK (India)
- PANKARARÉ.PAX (Brazil)
- PAPAVÔ.PPV (Brazil)
- PATAXÓ-HÃHÃHÃI.PTH (Brazil)
- PIJAO.PIJ (Colombia)
- POLARI.PLD (United Kingdom)
- QUINQUI.QUQ (Spain)
- RER BARE.RER (Ethiopia)
- SAKIRABIÁ.SKF (Brazil)
- SHOBANG.SSB (India)
- SININKERE.SKQ (Burkina Faso)
- TAPEBA.TBB (Brazil)
- TAUSHIRO.TRR (Peru)
- TINGUI-BOTÓ.TGV (Brazil)
- TRAVELLER SCOTTISH.TRL (United Kingdom)
- TREMEMBÉ.TME (Brazil)
- TRUKÁ.TKA (Brazil)
- UAMUÉ.UAM (Brazil)
- URARINA.URA (Peru)
- URU-PA-IN.URP (Brazil)
- WAKONÁ.WAF (Brazil)
- WAORANI.AUC (Ecuador)
- WARDUJI.WRD (Afghanistan)
- WASU.WSU (Brazil)
- WAXIANGHUA.WXA (China)
- WEYTO.WOY (Ethiopia)
- WUTANA.WUW (Nigeria)
- XINCA.XIN (Guatemala)
- YARÍ.YRI (Colombia)
- YARURO.YAE (Venezuela)
- YAUMA.YAX (Angola)
- YENI.YEI (Cameroon)
- YETFA.YET (Indonesia, Irian Jaya)
- YOKI.YKI (Indonesia, Irian Jaya)
- YUWANA.YAU (Venezuela)

Uralic (34)
- Finno-Ugric (28)
- - Finno-Permic (25)
- - - Finno-Cheremisic (22)
- - - - Cheremisic (2): MARI, HIGH.MRJ (Russia, Europe)
- - - - - MARI, LOW.MAL (Russia, Europe)
- - - - Finno-Mordvinic (20)
- - - - - Finno-Lappic (18)

- Balto-Finnic (9): ESTONIAN.EST (Estonia)
- - - - - - FINNISH.FIN (Finland)
- - - - - - INGRIAN.IZH (Russia, Europe)
- - - - - - KARELIAN.KRL (Russia, Europe)
- - - - - - LIV.LIV (Latvia)
- - - - - - LIVVI.OLO (Russia, Europe)
- - - - - - LUDIAN.LUD (Russia, Europe)
- - - - - - VEPS.VEP (Russia, Europe)
- - - - - - VOD.VOD (Russia, Europe)
- - - - - - Lappic (9)
- - - - - - Central (3): SAAMI, KILDIN.LPD (Russia, Europe)
- - - - - - - SAAMI, SKOLT.LPK (Russia, Europe)
- - - - - - - SAAMI, TER.LPT (Russia, Europe)
- - - - - - Eastern (1): SAAMI, INARI.LPI (Finland)
- - - - - - Northern (1): SAAMI, NORTHERN.LPR (Norway)
- - - - - - Southern (4): SAAMI, LULE.LPL (Sweden)
- - - - - - - SAAMI, PITE.LPB (Sweden)
- - - - - - - SAAMI, SOUTHERN.LPC (Sweden)
- - - - - - - SAAMI, UME.LPU (Sweden)
- - - - Mordvinic (2): ERZYA.MYV (Russia, Europe)
- - - - - MOKSHA.MDF (Russia, Europe)
- - - Permic (3): KOMI-PERMYAK.KOI (Russia, Europe)
- - - - KOMI-ZYRIAN.KPV (Russia, Europe)
- - - - UDMURT.UDM (Russia, Europe)
- - Ugric (3)
- - - Hungarian (1): HUNGARIAN.HNG (Hungary)
- - - Ob Ugric (2): KHANTY.KCA (Russia, Asia)
- - - - MANSI.MNS (Russia, Asia)
- Samoyedic (6)
- - Northern Samoyedic (3): ENETS.ENE (Russia, Asia)
- - - NENETS.YRK (Russia, Asia)
- - - NGANASAN.NIO (Russia, Asia)
- - Southern Samoyedic (3): KAMAS.XAS (Russia, Asia)
- - - MATOR.MTM (Russia, Asia)
- - - SELKUP.SAK (Russia, Asia)

Uru-Chipaya (2): CHIPAYA.CAP (Bolivia)
- URU.URE (Bolivia)

Uto-Aztecan (60)
- Northern Uto-Aztecan (12)
- - Hopi (1): HOPI.HOP (USA)
- - Numic (6)
- - - Central (2): COMANCHE.COM (USA)
- - - - SHOSHONI.SHH (USA)
- - - Southern (2): KAWAIISU.KAW (USA)
- - - - UTE-SOUTHERN PAIUTE.UTE (USA)
- - - Western (2): MONO.MON (USA)
- - - - PAIUTE, NORTHERN.PAO (USA)
- - Takic (4)
- - - Cupan (3)
- - - - Cahuilla-Cupeno (2): CAHUILLA.CHL (USA)
- - - - - CUPEÑO.CUP (USA)
- - - - Luiseno (1): LUISEÑO.LUI (USA)
- - - Serrano-Gabrielino (1): SERRANO.SER (USA)
- - Tubatulabal (1): TÜBATULABAL.TUB (USA)
- Southern Uto-Aztecan (48)
- - Aztecan (28)
- - - General Aztec (27)
- - - - Aztec (27): NAHUATL, CENTRAL PUEBLA.NCX (Mexico)
- - - - - NAHUATL, CENTRAL.NHN (Mexico)
- - - - - NAHUATL, CLASSICAL.NCI (Mexico)
- - - - - NAHUATL, COATEPEC.NAZ (Mexico)
- - - - - NAHUATL, DURANGO.NLN (Mexico)
- - - - - NAHUATL, GUERRERO.NAH (Mexico)
- - - - - NAHUATL, HUASTECA, EASTERN.NAI (Mexico)
- - - - - NAHUATL, HUASTECA, WESTERN.NHW (Mexico)
- - - - - NAHUATL, HUAXCALECA.NHQ (Mexico)
- - - - - NAHUATL, ISTHMUS, COSOLEACAQUE.NHK (Mexico)

- Galela-Loloda (3): GALELA.GBI (Indonesia, Maluku)
- - - - LABA.LAU (Indonesia, Maluku)
- - - - LOLODA.LOL (Indonesia, Maluku)
- - - Kao River (3): KAO.KAX (Indonesia, Maluku)
- - - - MODOLE.MQO (Indonesia, Maluku)
- - - - PAGU.PGU (Indonesia, Maluku)
- - - Sahu (4): GAMKONORA.GAK (Indonesia, Maluku)
- - - - IBU.IBU (Indonesia, Maluku)
- - - - SAHU.SUX (Indonesia, Maluku)
- - - - WAIOLI.WLI (Indonesia, Maluku)
- - - Tobaru (1): TABARU.TBY (Indonesia, Maluku)
- - - Tobelo (2): TOBELO.TLB (Indonesia, Maluku)
- - - - TUGUTIL.TUJ (Indonesia, Maluku)
- - - West Makian (1): MAKIAN, WEST.MQS (Indonesia, Maluku)
- - South (2): TERNATE.TFT (Indonesia, Maluku)
- - - TIDORE.TVO (Indonesia, Maluku)

Witotoan (6)
- Boran (2): BORA.BOA (Peru)
- - MUINANE.BMR (Colombia)
- Witoto (4)
- - Ocaina (1): OCAINA.OCA (Peru)
- - Witoto Proper (3)
- - - Minica-Murui (2): HUITOTO, MINICA.HTO (Colombia)
- - - - HUITOTO, MURUI.HUU (Peru)
- - - Nipode (1): HUITOTO, NIPODE.HUX (Peru)

Yanomam (4): NINAM.SHB (Brazil)
- SANUMÁ.SAM (Brazil)
- YANOMÁMI.WCA (Brazil)
- YANOMAMÖ.GUU (Venezuela)

Yenisei Ostyak (2): KET.KET (Russia, Asia)
- YUGH.YUU (Russia, Asia)

Yukaghir (2): YUKAGHIR, NORTHERN.YKG (Russia, Asia)
- YUKAGHIR, SOUTHERN.YUX (Russia, Asia)

Yuki (2): WAPPO.WAO (USA)
- YUKI.YUK (USA)

Zamucoan (2): AYOREO.AYO (Paraguay)
- CHAMACOCO.CEG (Paraguay)

Zaparoan (7): ANDOA.ANB (Peru)
- ARABELA.ARL (Peru)
- AUSHIRI.AUS (Peru)
- CAHUARANO.CAH (Peru)
- IQUITO.IQU (Peru)
- OMURANO.OMU (Peru)
- ZÁPARO.ZRO (Ecuador)

Bibliography

Agard, Frederick B. 1984. A course in Romance linguistics, Vol. 2: A diachronic view. Washington D.C.: Georgetown University Press.

Aschmann, Richard P. 1993. Proto Witotoan. Summer Institute of Linguistics and the University of Texas at Arlington Publications in Linguistics 114. Dallas.

Bright, William, ed. 1992. International Encyclopedia of Linguistics. New York: Oxford University Press.

Cloarec-Heiss, France. 1978. Étude preliminaire à une dialectologie banda. Études Comparatives. BSELAF 65. Paris: SELAF 65:11–42.

Clouse, Duane. n.d. A reconstruction and reclassification of the Lakes Plain languages of Irian Jaya. Submitted to Pacific Linguistics.

Grimes, Joseph E. 1989. Interpreting sample variation in intelligibility tests. In Thomas J. Walsh, ed. 1989. Synchronic and diachronic approaches to linguistic variation and change (Georgetown University Round Table on Languages and Linguistics 1988). Washington D.C.: Georgetown University Press, pp. 138-146.

———. 1995. Language survey reference guide. Dallas: Summer Institute of Linguistics.

Hopkins, Bradley Lynn. 1995. Contribution à une étude da la syntaxe Diola-Fogny. Ph.D. Thesis. Dakar: Université Cheikh Anta Diop de Dakar.

Tryon, Darrell T., ed. 1995. Comparative Austronesian dictionary: An introduction to Austronesian studies. Berlin: Mouton de Gruyter.